Church, State and Establishment

Paul Avis is General Secretary of the Council for Christian Unity of the Church of England. Previously he was a parish priest in the Diocese of Exeter. As Prebendary and Sub Dean of Exeter Cathedral and Research Fellow in the Department of Theology of the University of Exeter, he serves as Director of the Centre for the Study of the Christian Church. He has been a member of the Church of England Doctrine Commission and vice-chairman of the Faith and Order Advisory Group and has served on the General Synod. Dr Avis' books include *Faith in the Fires of Criticism: Christianity in Modern Thought* (Darton, Longman & Todd, 1995), *God and the Creative Imagination: Metaphor, Symbol and Myth in Religion and Theology* (Routledge, 1999) and *The Anglican Understanding of the Church* (SPCK, 2000). He is editor of *Divine Revelation* (Darton, Longman & Todd, 1997). He and his wife Susan have three sons and live in London and North Devon.

CHURCH, STATE AND ESTABLISHMENT

Paul Avis

Published in Great Britain in 2001 by
Society for Promoting Christian Knowledge
Holy Trinity Church
Marylebone Road
London NW1 4DU

British Library Cataloguing-in-Publication Data

A catalogue record for this book is available from the British Library

ISBN 0-281-05404-5

Typeset by David Gregson Associates
Printed in Great Britain by
Antony Rowe Ltd, Chippenham, Wiltshire

Contents

Preface   vii

1   The Church Embodied   1
2   The Idea of a National Church   11
3   The Meanings of Establishment   18
4   The Sovereign, the Church and the Constitution   23
5   The Lost Language of Church and State   37
6   The English Anglican Tradition on Church and State   45
7   Church, State and Modern Pluralism   63
8   Towards a United National Church in Mission   74

Bibliography   92

Index   99

Preface

Our focus in this book is on the relation between Church and State in principle and on the particular instance of this, colloquially known as the 'establishment' of the Church of England. But the motive and dynamic is thoroughly missiological. I will be asking such questions as: What does it mean to be a truly national Church with a nationwide mission of service and witness? Is this a monopoly of the Church of England and the Church of Scotland in Britain? What sort of relationship between Church and State has theological integrity? What is really meant by that much abused word 'establishment'? How many different models of 'establishment' are there among the Christian traditions? Is the established status of the Church of England and the Church of Scotland a help or a hindrance to their mission? How might the relationship of the churches to civil society develop more ecumenically? What are the realistic hopes for churches united in a national mission?

CHURCH AND STATE

I believe that we have almost lost the language that the Church developed over the centuries to enable it to think theologically about its relation to the God-ordained institution of the State. There are no doubt complex reasons for the current distancing of Church and nation, Church and State. A major cause is the process of the secularization of culture that has undermined the public significance of religious practice and the public profile of the churches. A linked factor is the process of the pluralization of society, whereby the historic national church begins to take its place as one religious institution among many and its qualitative distinctiveness becomes toned down.

But the causes of this mutual alienation also include the pathology of militant, aggressive nationalism in the twentieth century, where national sentiment has sometimes become the vehicle of racism or of some other demonic ideology. The historic ideal of a partnership between Church and State, as two divinely ordained institutions, given for the well-being of humankind, has been further corroded by the collusion of the churches with such nationalistic regimes – whether that has taken the form of warmongering by some bishops of the Church of England in the First World War, the assimilation of Lutheranism to the Nazi regime in Germany in the 1930s, the concordats between the Holy See and the Fascist dictators, or the chauvinism of some national Orthodox churches. But in the Christian theological economy, abuse does not destroy use. Not all the historical expressions of an integral relationship between Church and State can be condemned as corrupt, though no doubt all have been imperfect.

As I have already hinted, I maintain that there is a fundamental missiological reason for revisiting the question of Church and State. There is a national, as well as a local and a regional, dimension to Christian mission. I am quite clear that these territorial (sociological or demographic, we might say) contexts provide simply the opportunity or occasion for the Church's mission, not the ground of it. Mission is grounded primarily in the *missio Dei*, the outworking of God's gracious purpose for the whole of God's creation. It is grounded derivatively in the God-ordained nature of the Church as one, holy, catholic and apostolic. But mission cannot happen without such contexts, such 'occasions'. Therefore, the possibility of an overt, recognized, mutually beneficial relationship or partnership between Church and State should be taken seriously.

I take some time in this book to recover some key elements of this lost language. I attempt to summarize the complex biblical picture. I then touch on medieval political thought, Luther, Calvin and modern Roman Catholic theology. But I spend most time on what I regard as the classical Anglican tradition – the theological articulation of the relation between Church and State in such thinkers as Hooker, Burke, Gladstone, Thomas Arnold, Coleridge, Maurice and Creighton.

Of course I recognize that times have changed enormously since the days of the Bible and even of our forebears in the faith. That is why I take the trouble to trace, step by step, the emergence of a *de facto* plural – and ideologically pluralist – society, from the seventeenth century to the present. I note the further paradigm shift from a pluralism of Christian communities to a pluralism of world faith communities (anticipated by the presence of Jews from Cromwellian times). I ask whether these changed circumstances negate what the Church has consistently taught about the relation which it has sought with the State. I propose a modulated interpretation of the Church–State relationship that maintains continuity with the Christian tradition, yet takes seriously our present pluralist context. That does not lead me to abandon the ideal of 'establishment' – far from it.

I see no reason to backtrack on what theologians have taught about the State's obligation to acknowledge God and Christian truth, to provide for the spiritual, as well as the material needs of its citizens and to protect and support the mission and ministry of the Church. I hold that this obligation still pertains in spite of far-reaching cultural changes and I recognize that it takes many forms that are still operative even in our supposedly secular world. I explore ways in which I believe the Church–State relation can make sense in England – in Britain – even in (especially in!) an ecumenical age. (From now on I use state without the capital S, except when discussing the principle or ideal of the Church–State relation.)

As a result of our amnesia with regard to the tradition, there is, I believe, a danger that we may misread the signs of the times. I think there is evidence that some are making precisely that mistake. To me, the signs do not point to ever-advancing secularization and ever-increasing distance between Church and state. Instead they suggest a trend towards the deeper involvement of all the churches, including those that historically have been most reserved about being linked to the state, in the structures of civil society.

As I argue later, the sovereignty of nation states may be compromised by globalization, but states are assiduously legislating (in the context of transnational political and economic realities) with undiminished intensity for the lives of communities, institutions and individuals. Whether we consider healthcare, education, housing policy or even industry and commerce, we find that the state is at the same time both one step removed from the sharp end of things and yet all-pervasive. States may delegate, but they also regulate. They may devolve, but they do not cease to control. The issue of sovereignty is very much alive in the British constitutional context.

In the British constitution, we may say, sovereignty is vested in the Queen in Parliament under God. That sovereignty impinges heavily on the way that individual citizens, whether Christians or not, conduct their lives and it impinges equally rigorously on societies or communities, such as churches. Like all institutions in civil society, the churches cannot avoid being deeply involved at the level of the state. I am afraid that those who think otherwise are deceiving themselves. To fight such involvement, on the grounds of misguided principles, risks marginalization and irrelevance. The churches, like all institutions in civil society, are inevitably implicated in a relationship to the state. They need a theology to guide them in this demanding relationship.

ESTABLISHMENT

The highly visible bits of the Church of England's historic, constitutional relation to the state that people tend to get excited about are, in my view, not the most important. They are simply the cherry on the cake. Issues to do with the Crown's involvement in ecclesiastical appointments, how many bishops there should be in a 'reformed' Second Chamber, and the legislative competence of the General Synod in relation to Parliament are merely the ripples on the surface of the deep. I am entirely happy to defend most aspects of these arrangements as they stand. I am aware of few well-informed, principled objections to them. When they are seen in their historical perspective and constitutional context they are better understood.

But it is the submerged nine-tenths of the iceberg that is really important: the principle of partnership in service between Church and civil society; the national pastoral mission of the Church that aims to reach the whole community, territorially understood; the state's recognition of the things of God and its responsibility for the spiritual welfare of its citizens, in preference to a purely secular constitution; the acknowledged role of the Church in the debate over public issues. It is these things, rather than the other more contingent matters, that form the substantial content of 'establishment'.

'Establishment' is a word that has led many astray. It has almost come to be assumed – without proper investigation – that establishment is barely defensible. By the same token, what would probably be involved in 'disestablishment' (assuming that could be defended as a viable option) needs much more considered handling than it often receives. The terms establishment and disestablishment are a minefield. They need careful unpacking. My position may be dubbed by some 'antidisestablishmentarianism'. There is a certain mild satisfaction in being associated with the longest (or what was until recently the longest) word in the language. But my concerns go well beyond what is usually understood by that portentous word. They are theological, ecclesiological and fundamentally missiological. Those are three more somewhat over-long words that I would feel entitled to throw at anyone who might wish to stereotype or trivialize the argument that I will be developing in this book.

But before we embark on these issues, concerned with the national and civil context of the Church's life and mission, it would seem to make sense at least to recognize that this is certainly not the only or even the most important context. It is also the moment to flag up the dynamic that drives this vision of a reunited national church – the twin dynamisms of mission and unity. These hints give us our cue for the first chapter.

ACKNOWLEDGEMENTS

I would like to thank several colleagues at Church House, Westminster for expert advice on particular points: Dr Martin Davie (who has kindly read the text in its penultimate draft and made several perceptive criticisms), Brian Hanson, Dr Colin Podmore and Ingrid Slaughter. The Bishop of Winchester, the Right Reverend Michael Scott-Joynt, was good enough to read and respond to some early material. I have had the opportunity to compare notes with Professor David Fergusson, whose published *Bampton Lectures on Church and State* are anticipated. Two Methodist colleagues, the ecumenical theologian David Carter and the legal historian Susan Howdle, have also been most helpful. However, I must of course take full responsibility for the opinions that are deployed in the following chapters.

I am acutely aware that my argument contains some rather sweeping assertions, not least with regard to social interpretation. I have had to presuppose work that I have done, but that is not shown here, on such areas as secularization, globalization and postmodernity. I hope that a further book will give me the opportunity to expound these themes and to relate them to the robust survival of Christian images and to the explosion of new expressions of spirituality in our society – and to relate all this to the pastoral and evangelistic task, the mission of the Church.

I am not presuming to speak for the Council for Christian Unity, the Archbishops' Council or the General Synod of the Church of

England. However, in so far as I defend the integrity of the Church of England's present relationship with the state and look towards a greater ecumenical sharing of the Church–State relationship, I believe that I am fully in tune with the most recent debate of the General Synod (July 1994), the Church of England's submission to the Wakeham Commission on the reform of the House of Lords, and the response made by the Archbishops of Canterbury and York in June 2000 to the proposals of that Commission.

Material from the chapters on the national mission of a united Church was given as the first Richard Hooker Lecture, under the auspices of the Centre for the Study of the Christian Church, in Exeter Cathedral and at the University College of St Mark and St John, Plymouth, in November 1997. The material benefited from discussion at the Bristol Theological Society, meeting at Trinity College, Bristol, in February 1998. It was further refined by discussion at an academic consultation I was responsible for organizing on 'Church, State and Establishment' held at St George's House, Windsor Castle in April 1999 as part of the programme of the Centre for the Study of the Christian Church. Some of the material in this section of the book is summarized in my article 'Establishment and the Mission of a National Church' (*Theology*, Vol. CIII, No. 811, January/February 2000). I had the opportunity to test some material from Chapters Five and Six at the first meeting of the Church in Civil Society Seminar, again under the auspices of the Centre for the Study of the Christian Church, in November 2000.

Paul Avis

1

The Church Embodied

For most Christian people, the parish or the congregation is the hub of church life. Worship and fellowship within the immediate location circumscribes their experience of the Church. The strength of their Christian commitment is its rootedness, its loyalty to the local. They are, of course, aware of belonging to a wider church, in the first instance a deanery or a diocese, a circuit or a district – and beyond that to a church organized on a national or even international basis. But that tends to remain slightly academic. When they join in the creed at the Eucharist, they affirm a Church that is 'one, holy, catholic and apostolic', but they may have only a rather a hazy sense of what those numinous words mean.

Ecumenical theology is agreed about the broad meaning of these credal dimensions of the Church.

- *Unity* is given in our baptism into union with Christ through the power of the Holy Spirit (1 Corinthians 12.13) and in the fundamental baptismal trinitarian faith that we share ecumenically. But this given unity must be made visible and embodied – incarnated, so to speak – in structural form so that it becomes a visible witness to the gospel.
- *Holiness* belongs to God's calling of the Church, in the original biblical meaning of holiness as setting apart – setting apart by divine election to be the people of God with all the ethical implications of that (1 Peter 2). Though the holiness of the Church is far from perfectly realized in this world – the Church being always in need of repentance, reform and renewal – it is strengthened through the ministry of word and sacrament and through the discipleship effected by pastoral care and oversight.
- *Catholicity* is about the universal scope of salvation and the inclusiveness of the Church that is the unworthy instrument of

God's salvific purpose. Catholicity brings all nations and peoples within the fellowship of the Church and stands for the intimate connection between our life together as members incorporated into the mystical body of Christ and the life of natural, human community which is sanctified and ultimately transfigured by that connection. Therefore, all Christian churches see themselves as part of the Church catholic.

○ *Apostolicity* is the link between the definitive original message and mission of the Apostles whom Jesus Christ first commissioned and the tasks of the Church today. It refers to the dynamic continuity and spiritual faithfulness of the Church in mission. The fact that the essence of apostolicity is continuity with the Church of the Apostles has given rise to various interpretations. Forms of Roman and Anglican catholicism have seen the succession of episcopal consecrations of bishops and episcopal ordinations of clergy as an essential vehicle of apostolic continuity (hence the expression 'Apostolic Succession'). In reaction to this late medieval emphasis, the Reformers stressed continuity of true doctrine. Modern ecumenical theology has seen the apostolic continuity of the Church in terms of its faithfulness to the overall pattern of the Church of the Apostles, with its many facets, among which the handing on of the faith and the orderly transmission of authority have a key role.

We could summarize this understanding of the credal nature of the Church as 'mission-in-unity'. In Scripture and in the faith of the Church there is an indissoluble God-given connection between mission and unity, unity and mission. We need look no further than the *locus classicus* of the ecumenical movement (John 17.21) for this (see further below). The catholicity – reaching out to embrace all humanity – and the apostolicity of the Church – the dynamic of its mission – cannot be divorced from its unity and its fundamental calling to reflect the character of God (holiness).

The life of the Church for most Christians, together with its mission or outreach, is directed towards the local community, the immediate neighbourhood. But there are very good reasons why we need to expand our horizons and look beyond the parish or congregation if we are to grasp the true purpose or mission of the Church in the world – horizons that are required by its nature as one and catholic. These horizons are first extensive, to do with location and extent, and then intensive, to do with essential values that sustain the Church and are sustained by it. These values can be summarized under the rubric 'mission and unity'.

EXTENSIVE CONTEXTS

We can actually identify four extensive contexts or *loci* of the Church's unity and mission: parochial, diocesan, national (or provincial) and international or global. The first three of these terms are not meant to exclude those churches, such as the Methodist, Baptist and Reformed Churches, that do not normally operate in units of parishes, dioceses and provinces. They often have their equivalent structures (though it would achieve nothing to pretend that the major Christian churches in Britain share exactly the same ecclesiology, even where common ecclesiological principles can be discerned). For example, I make it clear when I come to discuss the mission of a 'national church' that this designation is a matter of degree. In a certain sense, a national ministry is not confined to the Church of England in England and the Church of Scotland north of the border. Let us glance briefly at each of these four contexts in turn.

Parochial

I want to touch base first of all with parochial ministry because Christian communities in the parishes are the fundamental building blocks of the Church. There is a distinctive pastoral ethos that belongs to churches, such as the Church of England and the Church of Scotland, that maintain a rich texture of territorial ministry, with church buildings in every significant community and a ministry to provide worship and pastoral care for all who are willing to receive it. The pastoral contact with individuals and families (not just the stereotyped nuclear family, of course) through ordained and recognized lay ministry in parishes – together with those institutional and *ad hoc* 'parishes' that comprise the sphere of pastoral ministry for chaplaincies (sector ministries) – constitutes the front line of the Church's mission. But in the broadly catholic understanding of the Church, including Anglican ecclesiology (see Avis, 2000), the parish and the worshipping congregation within it is not, strictly speaking, the normative unit of the Church. For that we need to enlarge our horizons a little.

Diocesan

The diocesan family, defined ecclesiologically, is the true 'local church' because it is the operative unit of oversight. The 'local church' is the community of word and sacrament (ultimately the eucharistic community) where the bishop is the chief pastor and the principal minister of word and sacrament and the cathedral is the mother church. Other traditions have their equivalent structures, based on their own particular sense of the fundamental unit of the Church. But for Anglicans, like Roman Catholics, Orthodox and members of other episcopally ordered churches, the diocese is the sphere or *locus* of the bishop's ministry.

By virtue of his office (not personality or style), which has a special orientation to unity and continuity, the diocesan bishop is the most fully representative minister, who gathers together the communities and their ministers into an ecclesial whole. The 'local church', in this ecclesiological sense, is the sphere in which the bishop, as the chief under-shepherd of the Lord, ministers word, sacrament and pastoral care and provides for them to be ministered through presbyters, deacons and authorized lay ministers of various kinds. No one, in an episcopally ordered church, has any authorized ministry without the bishop: he is ultimately responsible for the selection, training, ordination or commissioning, licensing, and oversight of all recognized ministers.

As an ecclesiological ideal, the diocese as local church stands for all baptized Christians ('all in each place'), united in service and witness under the leadership of the bishop and joined in fellowship through appropriate structures to every other local church ('all in every place'). The cathedral, with its distinctive ministry to those individuals and groups who slip through the net of the parochial structures, as well as its regular ministry to its own congregation, is the corresponding focal place of worship and teaching. A cathedral can be a magnet for the spiritual explorations of many who will not or cannot relate to the ministry provided in parishes. A mission-minded bishop will give unstinting support to the cathedral's unique outreach through its distinctive form of spiritual hospitality, as well as wanting to take every opportunity to use his episcopal seat as a base for teaching the faith. Anglican cathedrals and Westminster Abbey (perhaps also Westminster Cathedral), together with major historic parish churches, also have a national and international profile through the large numbers of modern pilgrims who come by car and coach for all their varied motives.

The church's unity and mission must, therefore, have wider horizons than the parish. Through its synod and the synod's boards and committees, the diocese, led by the bishop, provides vision, objectives, resources, support, supervision and accountability for ministry and mission. The pastoral skill and sensitivity that are requisite in the parish are just as necessary, magnified on a larger scale, in a diocesan-wide ministry. There are issues of policy and strategy, to do with resources, deployment and priorities, that need to be decided at the diocesan level.

National

However, a broader ecclesiological context than even the diocesan needs to be taken into account: the provincial or national context of the Church's unity and mission (in the Church of England, the two provinces of Canterbury and York make up the national church). Most Christian churches, since long before the Reformation, have been organized on a national basis and were even then in some sense (that I shall later elaborate) 'established'. At the Reformation, appeal was made to 'particular or national churches', in order to counteract the papal claim to universal jurisdiction over all churches, and their rulers assumed additional powers with regard to the protection and governance of the church in their lands. The relation between church and nation has been fundamental to Anglicanism and in their heyday the Nonconformist churches also had a strong sense of national responsibility and nationwide presence.

But nationhood is now undergoing some paradoxical changes. As a result of those economic, political and communications processes that comprise 'globalization', the autonomy or sovereignty of nations is being undermined. National boundaries are of diminishing economic and political importance. However, globalization is not all one-sided. Paradoxically, by reaction to global levelling, national and regional identities, often bound up with ethnic and religious loyalties and traditions, are experiencing a resurgence. It is arguable that, in a global perspective, the nation is more important now, in terms of collective identity, than ever before.

'Nation' is a flexible term. Are England, Scotland, Wales and Northern Ireland one nation or four? They are surely, in different senses, both. Well within living memory, but in a sense that is now anachronistic, King George VI spoke of the British Empire as a nation (James, 1998, p. 255). Ecclesial pluralism by nations long preceded denominational pluralism within nations.

The new factor in our national life is constitutional devolution in the United Kingdom, embodied in the Scottish Parliament, the Welsh Assembly, the devolved government that is available to Northern Ireland when the prior condition of peaceful agreement has been fulfilled, and the embryonic forms of regionalization in England, including London. But as devolution begins to take hold and make a difference to the lives of citizens in the four nations, the churches are increasingly gravitating towards each other in various unity conversations and through the ecumenical instruments Churches Together in Britain and Ireland, Churches Together in England, and various bodies at intermediate level. This convergence in the face of diversity and devolution is not another example of the churches being 20 years behind the times, but brings out the paradoxical character of what is happening to and between and within nations: globalization is matched by localization, disempowerment by reasserted identity, and fragmentation by new forms of community.

National churches (I mean primarily intensively territorial churches such as the Church of England and the Church of Scotland) intend to have a level of policy-making and government that has a nationwide perspective. They also mount a collective witness to the whole national community, minister to influential centres of power, and represent the values and hopes of a whole people. This aspect of the mission of national churches is considerably restricted in a largely pluralist society. However, the events surrounding the death of Diana Princess of Wales – when the churches found themselves caught up pastorally in an upsurge of inchoate religious feeling (whatever else it may have been) – show that it can be done.

A national church not only is committed to nationwide pastoral coverage, as it were, but also aims to project its message and values at every level of national structures and institutions. For the Church, that is simply an outworking of its mission (apostolicity) which knows no bounds (catholicity). Moreover, it typically looks for some form of tangible recognition from the focal centres of national life, some acknowledgement that its message and values are respected, honoured and taken seriously. Since it is divinely commissioned (Matthew 28.18–20) and speaks, for all its faults, in the name of the triune God, it can rest content with nothing less. When national commitment is met with national recognition (and it works the other way round too, when a Christian state lays pastoral obligations on the church of the nation), we talk of the establishment of the church in some sense.

International/global

Before we begin to tackle these topical and controversial issues to do with the national and established basis of the Church's mission, we need to note that the widening concentric circles of parish, diocese and national church broaden out even further to the global context. The much vaunted term globalization refers to economic, cultural and political developments that have the effect of weakening national boundaries and making everyone close neighbours. The churches approach this new and developing global context in three main ways.

First, the modern Roman Catholic Church is a global church with a strong central government located in the Vatican. It has not always been so but (to put the matter crudely but effectively) Ultramontanism – the progressive centralization of authority in Rome and the papal office – was the Roman Catholic Church's answer to the Protestant Reformation, Gallicanism, the Enlightenment, nineteenth-century nationalism, twentieth-century atheistic ideologies and various spontaneous forms of inculturation. Today the Roman Catholic Church tends to be unresponsive to regional, ethnic and national distinctions and aspirations; and the question of how far inculturation should go, without escaping the control of the central magisterium (authoritative teaching office), is a live issue. The Roman Catholic Church is an exception to the national organization of Christian churches, though it is very willing to enter into special relationships with sovereign states through concordats with the Holy See (see further below).

Second, the Christian world communions have emerged during the past century and a half but have become more closely co-ordinated and more effective in the past 50 years. The sense of an Anglican Communion (rather than a Church of England with imperial outposts) goes back to the mid-nineteenth century (see Sachs, 1993; Jacob, 1997) and the World Alliance of Reformed Churches stems from 1875. The Baptist World Alliance began in 1905 but first inaugurated global programmes after the Second World War. The Lutheran World Federation was founded in the aftermath of the

Second World War. International ecumenical dialogues, such as those between Roman Catholics and Lutherans and between Anglicans and Roman Catholics (ARCIC), have set the pace for bilateral progress towards Christian unity.

Third, international and regional ecumenical instruments, such as the World Council of Churches and the Conference of European Churches, and agreements such as the Leuenberg Concordat (between European Protestant churches) and the Porvoo Agreement (between the British and Irish Anglican and the Nordic and Baltic Lutheran churches), though they do not include the Roman Catholic Church, have been crucial in enlarging the boundaries of church life and mission beyond the national.

Since the focus of this book is on the relation of mission and service between church and nation, it seemed appropriate to acknowledge other contexts first: both those that are more local (the diocese and parish) and those that have wider horizons (the international and global). The nature of the Church of Christ, as one, holy, catholic and apostolic, means that it can never become assimilated to narrow national prejudices and ambitions, but must always retain its critical, prophetic independence.

The Church is called to witness and service within a national community. It characteristically seeks various partnerships with civil society. With due safeguards, it tends to welcome the state recognition of the Christian faith through some 'established', constitutional status and gladly accepts the pastoral obligations that this formal recognition brings. But the 'bottom line' for the Church is always that it is the Body of Christ, one, holy, catholic and apostolic. Nothing that I go on to claim for a 'national' church or for the opportunities of 'establishment' is intended to detract from that for one moment.

INTENSIVE CONTEXTS

The intensive or constitutive context of the Church's existence is comprised in the twin themes of mission and unity, or mission-in-unity. For nearly a century, mission and unity have been intimately linked in the thinking of the churches. It was when the modern missionary movement was at its peak, at the turn of the nineteenth century, and when the slogan 'The evangelization of the world in this generation' was coming into vogue, that the conscience of Christians involved in mission began to be smitten on account of the divisions within the Church. It was borne in upon Christian leaders that, while the churches were in a state of rivalry, competition and even sometimes outright opposition, the credibility of the gospel was undermined, not least on the mission field, but also at home, and the Lord Jesus Christ was dishonoured. The international missionary conference of Edinburgh 1910 brought together for the first time, on a world scale, the twin concerns of mission and unity and demonstrated their connection.

Recent ecumenical agreements bind unity and mission closely together. The report of the informal conversations between the Church of England and the Methodist Church, *Commitment to Mission and Unity*, makes the connection in this way:

> *The Gospel message of communion with God, with one another and with the world is compromised by our divisions, and consequently our witness to reconciliation is undermined … The continuing divisions between our churches give an ambiguous message to a society which is itself divided in many ways.*
>
> (*Commitment to Mission and Unity*, para. 43)

The report goes on to comment that 'the lack of unity at the national level prevents local churches from realizing their potential and from making their full contribution to the mission and catholicity of the Church'. Local ecumenical initiatives, 'which are in the vanguard of witnessing to a reconciled and reconciling life', need the authority and support that would come from a national agreement (para. 44).

The report of the Anglican–Methodist International Commission, *Sharing in the Apostolic Communion*, shows that there is a reciprocal relationship between mission and unity; they promote each other: 'We acknowledge that mission is both empowered by God's gift of unity within the Church and implements and makes visible the Church's unity for the world to see and believe' (Anglican–Methodist International Commission, 1996, para. 37).

The Methodist Conference statement on ecclesiology, *Called to Love and Praise* (1999), perceptively links mission and unity by grounding them both in the nature of God: 'The unity of the Church and its mission are closely related, since the Triune God who commissions the Church is One, seeking to reconcile and bring the world itself into a unity in Christ' (para. 3.2.1).

Mission and unity are bound together in God's single, undivided purpose to reconcile and unify all things through Christ (Ephesians 1.10). The two interconnected movements of this *missio Dei* are sending and gathering, mission and unity. The movement of sending out into the world is for the purpose of gathering in to the Church. Neither can happen without the other. The relatedness and the tension between them are grounded in the trinitarian action of God which embraces both these movements (cf. Raiser, 1999).

The argument of this book is concerned with mission-in-unity. It explores the timely question of the possibility of a united national church, in which the Church of England and the Nonconformist churches (in the first instance, probably the Methodist Church) would be united in a pastoral and prophetic mission to the nation in every part and at every level, while those churches with whom the prospects of full visible unity are considerably more distant (the Roman Catholic and Orthodox churches and those churches within the Baptist Union of Great Britain), are encouraged to share in this new stage of unity in mission as far as is practicable. The nature of the Church of Christ, as one, holy, catholic and apostolic, demands a vision of churches united in their national mission.

2

The Idea of a National Church

Two fundamental aspects of the modern world, the world that has come into being in the West since the early Enlightenment in the second half of the seventeenth century – secularization and pluralism – have long raised the question of the place of the Christian Church in the life of the nation. Let me pause to offer a working definition of these terms, conscious that I really need to say much more.

The term 'secularization' is often loosely used to suggest that people generally are less religious, less spiritual than they once were and that organized religion is destined to die out. Properly speaking, however, secularization refers to the gradual erosion of the public standing, authority and influence of the churches. In this sense, secularization has immediate relevance to our argument. What becomes of a national church whose role in national life seems to have moved from the centre to the periphery?

The term 'pluralism' refers to the other side of the coin. Even where public religion has been somewhat marginalized (secularization), an emerging plurality of faith communities further relativizes the role of all churches in society. When several organized faiths require some kind of acknowledgement by the state (for the state must must take cognisance of them as significant elements within society), what becomes of the national church that has been recognized in a particular and strong way because of its position in national life (i.e., it is 'established')?

So secularization and pluralism seem to challenge the historic role of national churches. But there are contrary indicators too. The momentous national response to the death of Diana, Princess of Wales, and the role played by the churches, and particularly by the Church of England (through the funeral service at Westminster Abbey), gave added point and urgency to the question of the mission of a national church and placed the whole matter in a different light for many reflecting people within the churches.

Besides this, the Labour Government of Tony Blair looks for the support of the churches in strengthening the sense of civic responsibility throughout the nation. At the time of the 1997 General Election that brought the Labour Party into office, the Roman Catholic Church in England and Wales anticipated this desire for partnership on the part of government by publishing *The Common Good*, which applied a coherent tradition of Roman Catholic social teaching to the problems of Britain today.

There is a widespread and largely unchallenged assumption that there is no sound theological justification for the role of the Church of England in the life of the nation on the present historic and constitutional basis – 'establishment' for short. In an essay on the Royal Supremacy, Gary Bennett concluded that the only justification for establishment today was a pragmatic one: it had advantages over the secular alternative (Bennett, 1988, p. 59). On the contrary, I want to insist that there are substantial theological principles, grounded in the nature of Church and state, that – though presupposed by theologians until recently, are often overlooked today – form the basis of a solid positive case for 'establishment'.

As far as the state is concerned, these principles have to do with such issues as: the profoundly biblical theme of the diverse callings of nations in the purposes of God; the historic role of Christian civilization in eliciting a sense of nationhood in medieval Europe; the duty of the state to be concerned for the spiritual welfare of its citizens; the importance of some formal and structural recognition of the things of God in the constitution of the state; the possibility of a Christian receiving from God a vocation or calling to a ministry in civil affairs; the accountability of state office holders to God for how they discharge their duties; the need for the state to honour those institutions within civil society, such as the churches, that make a valuable contribution to the social, moral and spiritual well-being of the community.

As far as the Church is concerned, these arguments include the earthed, territorial character of the Church's ministry when it is most effective; its deep pastoral involvement in the life of the community – and not just on its own terms in a take-it-or-leave-it manner; the legally recognized role of its pastors, the bishops and parish clergy, in the communities in which they are placed (dioceses and parishes) and the opportunities for witness and service that this brings; the institutional or structural channels that are needed for its mission of proclaiming the gospel of God, administering the sacraments of the Church, and teaching Christian faith and morals; the platform that the Church requires in order not to be marginalized and ignored but to contribute effectively to public doctrine (the values, priorities and other assumptions that govern public policy); the right to be critical in a prophetic way, which has to be earned by deep engagement and service.

These two lists are not exhaustive, just a few pointers, but perhaps they are sufficient to suggest straight away that the assumption that there are no important theological, ecclesiological or missiological principles at stake in the matter of 'establishment', made in good faith by so many who ought to know better, is deeply incoherent and deserves to be shot to pieces. My task in all that follows will be to try to substantiate this claim and to propose a cogent, credible rationale for the national mission of a Christian Church that is both united and in some sense 'established'. I begin by exploring the meaning of a 'national church'.

In a partly secularized, pluralist society, the definition of a national church is not straightforward. Several mainstream churches may feel that they have a mission to the whole nation. There may be degrees to which churches approximate to national churches. But it would be unrealistic to pretend that the future of a national church is not a matter of particular concern to established churches: Anglican in England, Presbyterian in Scotland. In an ecumenical age, it is no longer appropriate for the future of one church's mission (which is in any case the mission of God – *missio Dei*) to be considered without regard to the mission of other churches. As far as England is concerned, the issue might be regarded as a peculiarly Anglican question with an ecumenical answer.

The idea of a national church belongs to the essence of historical Anglicanism. It is integral to the Anglican understanding of the Church. The dominant concrete form of the Church recognized by historical Anglicanism is the national one. This emphasis goes back to the Reformation and the rise of the nation state, though it was gathering strength long before then. We should beware of setting church and nation in antithesis. The idea of nationhood is not in origin a secular concept. 'Its tradition began its life at the breast of Christianity.' Christian thought and the historical development of nationhood have been intertwined (Ernest Barker in Nicholls (ed.), 1967, pp. 156f).

The Thirty-Nine Articles refer to 'particular or national Churches' (Article XXXIV). This term relates to three central planks of Reformation theology: first, there is such a thing as a valid national expression of the catholic Church; second, a national church has the inherent authority to reform itself, even when the wider church resists the demand for reform; and third, all estates (or as we might say today, interests or constituencies) of the nation, including the laity, have a say in the governance of the national church. As Norman Sykes put it: 'The validity of the Anglican position depends upon the recognition of the right of national Churches to fashion their own doctrine, discipline, and organisation, and of the right of the laity to participate in the definition of matters of faith and order' ([Cecil], 1936, p.301).

However, the Anglican emphasis on the national church is not confined to the Church of England. The existence of the Anglican Communion assumes that there is a national expression of the Christian Church. Anglicanism has tended to define itself as a fellowship of national churches. It is not a single global church like the Roman Catholic Church, made up of local churches (dioceses) that look to a central authority (the papacy). It is a fellowship of legally autonomous yet spiritually and pastorally interdependent provinces (in some cases comprising more than one province) functioning as national churches, each constituted by dioceses and each having integrity as churches of Christ. The Lambeth Conference of 1930 stated that one of the distinguishing marks of those churches which make up the Anglican Communion is that 'they are particular or national Churches, and as such, promote within each of their territories a national expression of Christian faith, life and worship' (Resolutions 48 and 49: Coleman, 1992, pp. 83ff).

This historical Anglican position raises some questions for the smaller and newer Anglican provinces and it may be pertinent to ask whether they really see themselves as national churches. Some provinces, in West Africa, Central and South America or South East Asia, span several nations and are properly described as regional churches. (Strictly speaking, the same could be said of the Church of England, since it includes the Isle of Man, the Channel Islands and the Diocese of Gibraltar in Europe.) Many Anglican churches, including the Episcopal Church of the United States of America, the Church in Wales and the Scottish Episcopal Church, are minority churches. Clearly, size and majority status are not essential for national churches, though it is a moot point whether a church that is not able to extend itself throughout a nation, and makes only a modest impact on national life, can be truly described as a national church (though that can remain a legitimate aspiration). What then is the essence of a national church?

The idea of a national church is ambiguous. It can easily sound chauvinistic, as though it were an ethnic or nationalistic church that was meant. There is no doubt that in the past such a notion has been invoked to appeal to people's less elevated instincts. In the1874 General Election J. A. Roebuck defeated Joseph Chamberlain in Sheffield under the slogan 'The Briton's Bible and the Briton's Beer: our National Church and our National Beverage!' (McLeod, 1996, p. 98). I hope it goes without saying that neither an ethnic nor a nationalistic interpretation is being advocated here. Christianity cannot collude with national (especially ethnic) prejudices of a chauvinistic kind or allow itself to become the tool of a state ideology or national myth. (For an account of the role of national feeling, patriotism and royalty in British religion, see Wolfe, 1994.) My argument does not appeal to 'Englishness' (whatever that may mean today) nor even to nationality, and only in a muted way to any sense of national identity. Nevertheless, given that proviso, it remains true that, in most circumstances that are likely to arise, a faith that persistently stands in contradiction to national identity is in danger of being driven into a sterile sectarianism. A national church, therefore, is stamped with national cultural identity and sees its mission as being to the national community that has left its mark upon it (cf. Martin, 1993, p. 101). Nevertheless, in terms of Christian ecclesiology, it is a genuine expression of the one Church of Christ: it is nothing less than the Church – and that alone is non-negotiable.

The idea of a national church, as I will defend it, is of a church that is concerned with a nationwide mission of the gospel and nationwide service to the community. A national church understands that its mission is to the whole nation, to the whole population considered as a great community (or a community of communities). It is committed to providing its ministry of word, sacrament and pastoral care to every section of the population. It has a close and sympathetic relationship to national culture and, more locally, to regional expressions of that culture. It has a chaplaincy role to national institutions, such as schools and colleges, municipal corporations, the armed services, hospitals and penal institutions. It expects to make its contribution to the articulation of public doctrine, particularly in social and educational policy and to the principles of wide acceptance that underlie it. It aims to project its message, its values and its presence at every level of national life. Though it will be prepared to be prophetic and critical and to make judgements that will be unpopular, it will generally seek the middle ground and look for consensus. Critical solidarity is its hallmark. To illustrate this, not from the Church of England but from the Church of Scotland: the Articles of that established church declare it to be 'a national Church representative of the Christian faith of the Scottish people [which] acknowledges its distinctive call and duty to bring the ordinances of religion to the people in every parish of Scotland through a territorial ministry' (cf. Forrester, 1999, p. 84).

In theory the idea of a national church does not depend on legal establishment, though we should be aware that it may be dependent on endowment in order to maintain the national extension of its mission. It would still be open to a church, as a voluntary body, to commit itself, as a matter of strategy, to providing a place of worship and a pastoral ministry in every local community and to offer its ministrations to all who would receive them. But then, of course, if that proved impossible to sustain, it could withdraw (as, I believe, the English Protestant churches have in some cases felt compelled to withdraw from remote rural areas and in some cases from inner cities) and no one could gainsay it.

What is sometimes overlooked, however, in discussions on establishment is that it is not simply the national extension of the church that is involved, but the role of its clergy (especially bishops) in civil society. Only establishment – the recognition on the part of the state of the contribution of Christian ministry to the health of civil society – can provide a basis for the pastoral responsibility of the Church at large (see further below).

There is currently a good deal of uncertainty about the idea of a national church – in particular about the identity and mission of the Church of England. This uncertainty is related both to the increasing pluralism of society, in which the historic national church seems to be more and more simply one faith community among others, and to the increasing secularization of society, whereby religious commitment becomes more and more marginalized in terms of public assumptions and is increasingly relegated to the sphere of individual preference and private practice. But I sense that it also results from a weakening of the sense of the catholicity of the Church.

What, for want of a better word, can be called 'congregationalist' attitudes are rampant in some Church of England parishes. The local worshipping community is often seen as sufficient unto itself and not as dependent on a wider body or answerable to a higher authority. Reform of patronage law has given parishes a greater say in the choice of the parish priest. The growth of non-stipendiary ministry (especially ordained local ministry) has given them a greater role in calling public ministers. Substantial increases in parochial share, to pay for the stipendiary ministry, have strengthened the demand for control of how – and on whom – it is spent. Many church people have a weak perception of the diocese and the national church as expressions of the Church of Christ. Sometimes it is even suggested that the term 'The Church of England' is outmoded and arrogant (I do not know whether a similar suggestion has been made north of the border).

This loss of a wholeness of vision is based, at least partly, on a deficient ecclesiology. In truth it is the catholicity and the apostolicity of the Christian Church, not any prejudice or sentiment about nationality, that drives its mission to the whole of a people, a nation. Catholicity gives the momentum towards unity and inclusiveness. Apostolicity provides the momentum that stems from the mission of the Apostles and faithfulness to their message of salvation. The breadth and depth of God's saving purpose cannot be encompassed by merely congregational horizons.

3

The Meanings of Establishment

Few discussions suffer from as much mystification as arguments about 'establishment'. Much that is said and written about 'establishment' (and, by the same token, 'disestablishment') is fatally flawed by the assumption that 'establishment' is *one thing* – that a church is either established or not established. In truth, there is a wide range of possibilities for the relation of church and state that is embraced by the term establishment and comparisons are odious. There can be little meaningful comparison between the conditions of establishment in, say, the Church of Ireland in the mid-nineteenth century, before disestablishment, and the Church of England at the beginning of the twenty-first century. One hundred and fifty years of political, constitutional, social and theological change make such comparisons meaningless. There is sometimes a cavalier disregard for the contingencies of history and the complexities of the constitution when questions of establishment and disestablishment are discussed.

Even more objectionable is the use of these two portmanteau words as value judgements. If establishment were by definition bad and disestablishment good, as some seem to assume, nine-tenths of the relationships that the Christian Church has had with various states during the past two millennia would be condemned. Serious discussion is further bedevilled by the popular confusion between the Church of England by law established and the satirical, *Private Eye*, sense of 'The Establishment' – meaning not so much the great and the good as the pompous, the privileged and the out of touch. There is, as we say, no smoke without fire and it is not difficult to see how the confusion has arisen. However, some of the media capitalize on this confusion wilfully to obscure the issues. So let us now try to clarify some of the issues at stake.

First, it is perhaps worth pointing out that the original meaning of 'established', applied to the church or religion, was largely descriptive.

It meant 'settled', 'resolved', 'stabilized', following a period of political upheaval and instability, as in the so-called 'Elizabethan Settlement of religion'. The Latin underlying the phrase in the canons 'by law established' is *legibus stabilitam* (Bray, 1998, pp. 270ff; cf. Figgis, 1913, pp. 9ff). That does not mean that the English Church was not in practice established before the Reformation. The term 'establishment' will not bear the moral weight placed upon it by some advocates of disestablishment. 'Establishment' stands for a series of applied and therefore evolving connections between church and state (Carr, 1999). It is an imprecise, generic term that can be used of the relation of many churches in many countries to the state.

Second, there is an important distinction between an established church and a state church. An established church is not necessarily a state church, though it may be. In the strict sense of a state church, where national and religious identity coincide and national government and church government are one and the same, the Church of England has never been a state church. Before and after the Reformation the Convocations had their own legislative authority. In the formative period of the Church of England, the presence of Separatists, recusant Roman Catholics and later Jews undermined Hooker's vision of a Christian commonwealth and subverted the desire of monarchs and bishops for complete religious uniformity. In a looser sense, the Church of England has not been a state church since 1828–31 when its legal, civic monopoly was broken (see next chapter). In 1919 it achieved virtual self-government (delegated by Parliament). Its doctrine, worship and discipline are not controlled by the state legislature. Its places of worship are not maintained by the state. Its clergy and bishops are not salaried by the state nor is their training supervised by the state. Let us take a topical example of the distinction between a state church and an established church.

It is understandable that the Church of Sweden is now welcoming a substantial measure of disestablishment (see Persenius, 1999). Until recently the Church of Sweden was a state church. Until 1996 one did not even have to be baptized to be a member. The 'new relationship' (as it is felicitously referred to) between the Church of Sweden and the Swedish state will strengthen the integrity of the church by grounding membership in baptism and will actually enhance its mission as an impressive nationwide pastoral visitation is made to explain to families the privileges and responsibilities of membership and to extend an invitation to parents to bring their children for baptism. To the Swedes what is happening may seem like disestablishment, but 'partial disestablishment' or, better still, a 'new relationship with the state' seems a more appropriate description.

There are several reasons for this. First, it is precisely by the action of the state, through the Church of Sweden Act, that the church will gain substantial autonomy. Second, it will be singled out in a salient way in the constitution. Third, it will have a statutory responsibility for burial places for the whole nation. Fourth, its work will continue to be partly financed through a church 'fee' (rather than tax, as before) which will be collected by the state administration. Fifth, the monarch will continue to be a Lutheran and is described as 'the first member' of the Church of Sweden. Clearly, in English terms, the Church of Sweden is very far from having been disestablished.

What is remarkable is not that the Church of Sweden is loosening its ties with the state, but that the Free Churches in Sweden will be brought into a closer relationship with the state through compulsory registration and voluntary participation in the church fee mechanism. Clearly some degree of state recognition and state involvement is not an issue between the Swedish Free Churches and the Church of Sweden. The same dynamic is at work in Britain as the non-established churches are being drawn into participation in a reconstituted Second Chamber of Parliament.

Third, establishment implies a formal relation between the monarch and the established church. The Queen is Anglican in England and Presbyterian in Scotland. But a church may be established by law and the sovereign not have any powers other than those she possesses as head of state. The Queen does not have the same role in the established Church of Scotland as she does in the Church of England. Though she is formally represented, with some considerable ceremony, at its General Assembly, she is not Supreme Governor (even in a constitutionally nuanced way) and does not appoint its chief ministers (even nominally). I will shortly be attempting to demonstrate the high degree of mutual implication between the established church and the monarchy in the British constitution, but at this stage it is useful to recognize that they are theoretically separate issues.

Fourth, establishment may entail a role for church leaders (usually bishops) in the legislature, though it does not require it. The place of bishops in the House of Lords is not an effect of the Reformation settlement. Bede's *Ecclesiastical History of the English Nation* and the *Anglo-Saxon Chronicle* show bishops taking their place in the councils of kings before there was even a unified kingdom in England. They sat in the House of Lords from its inception, long before the

Reformation. The Bishop of Winchester's predecessor in the see served Alfred the Great. It belongs to their proper ministry as chief pastors in a nation that acknowledges Christianity.

If the representation of Church of England bishops in the Second Chamber were significantly to be reduced (or even abolished altogether), the establishment of the Church of England would not be affected in principle (cf. Lewis-Jones, 1999). Leaders of the established Church of Scotland do not sit in the Lords by virtue of office. The British Government has recently raised that possibility in its white paper on the future of the Second Chamber, and the Church of Scotland, in its response, has not ruled it out. If the non-established churches take up the offer of representation in the Second Chamber, they will be moving to a closer relationship to the state – a kind of creeping establishment.

Fifth, establishment takes many forms. There are shades and degrees of establishment. It is not a univocal concept. But at its lowest establishment involves some kind of recognition of a church by the state and corresponding obligations on the part of the church. There are churches that are 'strongly' established, such as the Church of Denmark which has no synodical machinery distinct from the state legislature. In Finland there are two established churches of very unequal size, the Lutheran and the Orthodox. The doctrinal confession and the legal constitution of both are laid down by the state.

Even in those countries where a legal separation of church and state has taken place, there are often arrangements negotiated between the two that savour of establishment. For example, in Belgium the salaries, housing and pensions of the clergy and ministers of various faiths (not only Christian denominations) are provided by the state. In Germany there is a guaranteed public role for the churches, a church tax or fee and confessional theological faculties in state universities. Even in France, where the separation of church and state might be thought to be particularly rigorous, the state owns Roman Catholic churches built before 1905 and undertakes major repairs to them. Some avowedly secular states require churches to register and this can entail the state defining what is meant by church membership.

In Britain both the Methodist Church and the United Reformed Church, in their present forms, were constituted under parliamentary enabling legislation. The legal basis on which the Methodist Conference exercises its oversight is an act of Parliament. The Roman Catholic hierarchy operates under some form of recognition or permission on the part of the state (Robbers (ed.), 1996; Doe, 1996, pp. 7–11).

Finally, let us return to the Anglican aspect. It is often said that the Church of England is the only church of the Anglican Communion that is established. Though strictly true, this statement is rather misleading. Doe significantly claims that no Anglican church is established in the full sense (for what follows, see Doe, 1998, pp. 13ff). Within the Anglican Communion there is considerable diversity in the relation of the provinces to their host states. The 1930 Lambeth Conference (Resolution 52) encouraged provinces to form into national churches and left open the question of stronger links with the state. 'Saving always the moral and spiritual independence of the divine society, the Conference approves the association of dioceses or provinces in the larger unit of a "national church", with or without the formal recognition of the civil government' (Coleman (ed.), 1992). There are several quasi-established Anglican churches, such as some provinces of the Church of Canada and of the Church of Australia. These have close legal links with the state. The authority of their canon law rests, at least in part, on secular legislation and secular legislation expressly and directly regulates some of the temporal affairs of those churches. Then there are those Anglican churches whose legislative competence in their own sphere is recognized expressly by the law of the land (Wales, Ireland, Bermuda and Barbados) or awarded by Royal Licence (New Zealand).

Furthermore, where Anglican churches have been disestablished, the legislative process has left a lasting imprint on the constitutions of those churches. The Irish Church Act of 1869 laid down that the prevailing laws and doctrines of the established church should be binding in the disestablished church, unless subsequently altered by the church. A similar arrangement was provided for the Church in Wales by the Welsh Church Act of 1914. Where Anglican churches are unestablished, in the sense that they never have been established, this is often in countries (especially in Central and South America) where the Roman Catholic Church is established by virtue of concordats with the Holy See (see next chapter).

4

The Sovereign, the Church and the Constitution

Let us now consider further the relevance of the monarchy to the idea of a national church and to the question of establishment. We need to consider, at this point, any misgivings on the part of the Church of England's ecumenical partners – and even on the part of some Anglicans – to aspects of this complex of constitutional arrangements and to see whether these can be allayed.

The doctrine of the Royal Supremacy was constructed in the 1530s to safeguard the unity and integrity of the realm. Ultimately it was for national self-defence. It reduced the two sovereignties, two jurisdictions, that of the king and that of the Pope – a dualism that had become intolerable – to a single sovereignty or jurisdiction. 'The Henricean statutes, by restraining appeals to Rome and by converting the canon law into the King's ecclesiastical law, restored a unified jurisdiction to the realm: the Sovereign became the fount of justice in causes spiritual as well as temporal' (Dunstan, 1982, p. 136).

This is the concern that underlies the frequently misunderstood assertion of the Thirty-Nine Articles that 'The Bishop of Rome hath no jurisdiction in this realm of England' (Article XXXVII). The legislation of Henry VIII's reign abolishing the jurisdiction of the Pope presupposed that 'this realm of England is an empire' (Elton, 1972, p. 344) – that is, autonomous and self-sufficient in authority – and that the realm constituted a 'congregation' or *ecclesia* of 'faithful men' (Article XIX) among whom the sovereign ruled. He or she had both temporal and ecclesiastical jurisdiction.

Under Elizabeth I, clergy had to take the oath of allegiance to the effect that 'the Queen's Highness is the only supreme governor of this realm . . . as well in all spiritual or ecclesiastical things or causes as temporal'. This legislation reflected the overriding priority of national security: to safeguard the integrity of the realm against foreign interference from the Pope and those European rulers who owed him allegiance, particularly Philip II of Spain. It insisted that 'No foreign prince, person, prelate, state or potentate hath or ought to have any jurisdiction . . . ecclesiastical or spiritual within this realm' (Elton, 1972, pp. 364ff).

The Royal Supremacy emerged historically as a counterbalance to the temporal aspirations of the papacy. In the late medieval period, canon law had attributed unlimited powers to the Pope, transferring (as Figgis frequently points out: Figgis, 1913, pp. 135ff) the omnipotence of late Roman emperors to the sphere of church authority. This amounted in the end to an idea of a universal papal monarchy which directly impinged on the authority of temporal rulers. If the monarch was a sacred figure, the Pope was a political force. Later distinctions between spiritual and temporal were blurred in the Reformation period.

The term 'Royal Supremacy' (i.e., sovereignty) needs to be nuanced somewhat today when applied to a constitutional monarchy. A constitutional monarch 'reigns but does not rule' (Hennessy, 1996, p. 50). Ultimate sovereignty is vested in the Crown. That is not to say that sovereignty originates in the Crown: it would probably be generally agreed that its source is ultimately in the people. (Burke distinguishes between where sovereignty originates and where it resides: Burke, 1834, p. 509.) The expression 'the Crown' I take to stand for the constitutional mediation of the authority of the monarch. The sovereign acts constitutionally, that is to say, through Parliament and her ministers, in ecclesiastical as well as in strictly political matters.

It is sometimes suggested that the parliamentary 'middle-man' could be cut out so that the sovereign could receive advice on church legislation, which requires the Royal Assent, or on ecclesiastical appointments directly from the church (say, via the Archbishops). It is true that there are a very small number of matters in which the sovereign acts without ministerial advice. (On the scope and limits of the constitutional authority of the sovereign, see Bagehot, 1963; Bogdanor, 1995; Hennessy, 1996. For a fascinating account of the political influence of the monarchy from William IV to George VI, see James, 1998.) However, the principle of 'ministerial responsibility' protects the sovereign from criticism to which he or she cannot reply. The sovereign cannot be called to the bar of Parliament to give account. The ministers of the Crown take responsibility for matters in which the sovereign is involved constitutionally. It seems right that the Ecclesiastical Committee of Parliament should scrutinize Measures emanating from the General Synod with special regard to the constitutional rights of the Queen's subjects under the law (for an account of the origins of this arrangement and a balanced assessment see Lord Bridge's Appendix V in [Bridge], 1997).

The principle of ministerial responsibility explains why, in my opinion, it is constitutionally inappropriate to suggest, as a recent report of the General Synod on senior appointments did, that the sovereign should nominate bishops on the immediate advice of the church, rather than on the advice of the Queen's First Minister. There is, however, a further weighty reason why the state cannot be uninvolved, albeit in a strictly circumscribed way, in the appointment of bishops and deans and in the approval of Measures emanating from the General Synod ('Measures' are sometimes used to give parliamentary permission for the Synod to proceed to legislate by canon in areas where it has not yet done so), and to this we now turn.

ESTABLISHMENT AND TERRITORIAL MINISTRY

The Church of England, by virtue of its distinctive ecclesiology enshrined in the law of the land, ministers to the whole population territorially, through the dioceses and parishes. It has a pastoral ministry to the community at large (provided, of course, that individuals are willing to receive its ministry) and a responsibility, awarded precisely by the state, for the spiritual welfare of citizens. In other words, it has a structural, constitutional place and role, recognized and committed to it by the state, in national life, and this provides one of the 'incarnational' channels through which its gospel mission as the Church of Christ is carried out.

'Every bishop is the chief pastor of all that are within his diocese, as well laity as clergy, and their father in God' (Canon C18). This doctrine of episcopal ministry is the theological basis of the cure of souls exercised by parochial clergy by the authority of the diocesan bishop. The question that needs to asked here is, 'Who says so?' The individual bishop does not arrive in his diocese and set himself up as chief pastor of everyone. So by what authority is the bishop chief pastor of clergy and laity in his diocese? Several strands need to be teased out here. There is the general principle and the particular case.

As to the general principle, it is a teaching (a doctrine) of the catholic Church, that the bishop is chief pastor of that portion of the people of God committed to the bishop's care and oversight. As to the particular case of the Church of England, the doctrine is enshrined in its canon law and *ipso facto* in the law of the land. Now let us consider the actual operation and carrying out of that pastoral ministry. What aspects come from the Crown, from the sovereign in Parliament?

Let us first of all be clear about what does not come from the Crown. The bishop's ministerial authority *(potestas ordinis)* to proclaim the gospel, teach the faith, administer the sacraments and provide pastoral oversight come from Christ as Lord and Head of the Church and from no other source. In their ministry of word, sacrament and pastoral oversight bishops represent Christ and the Church.

But it seems that there are two related aspects of episcopal oversight that can be traced back to the Crown, the source of all temporal authority. The first is the bishop's jurisdiction, that is, his legal authority that can be enforced in the courts because the law of the Church of England is part of the law of the land and ecclesiastical courts are the Queen's courts (Moore, 1967, p. 14). The second is the allocation of the bishop's see, the territorial and demographic delimitation of his oversight. Who decides that a bishop shall be chief pastor of one particular community of people, or section of the population? Who commits to a bishop the portion of the people of God, within a given territory, that is to be his care or cure? In constitutional terms only the Crown can award that responsibility. The territorial ministry and the office of bishop as chief pastor therein are connected to establishment. Otherwise, bishops would be chief pastors of a collection of congregations only and clergy would be merely chaplains to those congregations. That is not how they are seen or see themselves.

THE CROWN AND THE CHURCH TODAY

The executive role of the sovereign as Supreme Governor of the Church of England has been steadily eroded since the sixteenth century to a mere shadow of its former power. Constitutionally, since 1688 (and de facto since the outcome of the Civil War) it has been Parliament that has exercised ultimate sovereignty. However, the canon law of the Church of England still affirms that church and nation are united under the Crown. Canon A7, significantly entitled 'Of the Royal Supremacy', states that 'the Queen's excellent Majesty, acting according to the laws of the realm, is the highest power under God in this kingdom, and has supreme authority over all persons in all causes, as well ecclesiastical as civil'. What does this mean?

Ecclesiastical causes may be distinguished from the citadel of the heart. They do not impinge on conscience or transgress 'the law of Christ'. The person of the sovereign constitutionally and symbolically unifies the spiritual and temporal aspects of national life, but it is explicitly said that the sovereign acts according to the laws of the realm and these laws are made by Parliament and (be it noted) by the Church of England's own legislative body, the General Synod. That is why it is often said that it is the Queen-in-Parliament that is sovereign. Constitutionally, that sovereignty extends, in those ecclesiastical causes to which the law pertains, not only to the Church of England, but to the Protestant churches and the Roman Catholic Church (Doe, 1996, p. 32).

The Royal Supremacy, seen in historical perspective, should not be condemned as mere Erastianism (as G. V. Bennett rightly insisted: Bennett, 1988, p. 47). It did not and does not imply, as the term Erastian properly suggests, a separation between church and state with the state controlling the church's discipline. The sovereign was and is a member of the church. The person in whom the Royal Supremacy was embodied was inside, not outside, the church – and still is. (For a discussion of Erastianism, see Figgis, 1922, pp. 293–342.)

The headship claimed by Henry VIII and the supreme governorship exercised by Elizabeth and her successors was not one of holy order but of jurisdiction or legal oversight (see Elizabeth's *Injunctions*, 1559). It was not sacramental and did not infringe the spiritual ministry of the clergy. The Thirty-Nine Articles underline the distinction:

Where we attribute to the King's Majesty the chief government ... we give not to our Princes the ministering either of God's Word, or of the Sacraments ... but only that prerogative, which we see to have been given always to all godly Princes in Holy Scripture by God himself; that is, that they should rule all estates and degrees committed to their charge by God, whether they be Ecclesiastical or Temporal ...

(Article XXXVII)

Once again, the distinctions were blurred, for Henry toyed with the idea of ordaining bishops and saw himself as a sort of lay bishop, if not pope! Henry, Elizabeth, James I and Charles I all took a hand in the direction of doctrine. Hooker, notably, played down the authority of the supreme governorship, claiming that only the bishop's see, together with 'the profits, pre-eminences, honours thereunto belonging' (i.e. the temporalities) were received from the sovereign (Hooker, 1845, vol. 3, p. 419). Hooker also concedes a permissive authority on the part of the Crown, that has sovereignty over all subjects, that enables the bishop to exercise oversight over any citizen (p. 467). John Cosin, a Caroline divine par excellence, said of Charles I in 1628: 'King Charles is not Supreme Head of the Church of England under Christ, nor hath he any more power of excommunication than my man that rubs my horse's heels' (Collinson, 1982, p. 18). Van Mildert ('The Last of the Prince Bishops of Durham' and one of the last High Church defenders of the Anglican state) defined the power of order (*potestas ordinis*) as 'that power which confers the capability of exercising spiritual functions', i.e., to preach, baptize, administer the Eucharist, ordain, confirm and consecrate. This clearly was bestowed by Christ through the Church. The power of jurisdiction (*potestas iurisdictionis*), on the other hand, Van Mildert regarded as the authority to appoint 'particular persons to exercise spiritual functions throughout the state' and this power was derived from the state, though exercised by the church (Varley, 1992, p. 126). There is no question whatsoever, in Anglican formularies or writers, of the church's apostolic authority and that of its officers being bestowed by the state.

The essential distinction between power of order and power of jurisdiction is still preserved in the involvement of the Crown in the appointment of bishops. A brief look at two aspects of that involvement will substantiate the point.

The scope and limits of the role of the Crown in the appointment of a bishop to a see are nicely reflected in the words of the Royal Mandate which is read by the Provincial Registrar at the consecration of a suffragan bishop. (In the Church of England a bishop is consecrated to a see just as a deacon or priest is ordained to a parochial title.) The church makes known to the Crown the needs of a particular diocese where a vacancy has arisen and offers the names of two candidates who, in the church's judgement, meet the spiritual requirements of the position. Responding to that request, the Crown allocates one of the candidates put forward by the church to the see (by convention the first name is chosen). In the Royal Mandate the Crown then commends the candidate to the church for all due prayers and ceremonies that are required to make him a bishop. In the carefully chosen words of this document there seems to me to be a very nice and proper division of labour. I do not see that anyone, who understands the constitutional position of the monarch as the focus of sovereignty in the life of the nation, can take exception to it.

The Oath of Homage, made to the sovereign by every new diocesan bishop, refers to temporalities and spiritualities. The bishop acknowledges that he receives both these from the hand of Her Majesty. These terms are sometimes misunderstood, as though they transgressed the 'law of Christ' and created an issue of conscience. While it is assumed that 'temporalities' refers to the temporal appurtenances of the see (the bishop's residence, income, etc.), it is assumed that 'spiritualities' refers to the bishop's spiritual authority, that is to say, the power of order in word and sacrament. In fact both these terms have a restricted, technical meaning.

The only temporality for which the Queen is still responsible during the vacancy is the power of patronage to livings of which the bishop is patron by virtue of his see – the bishop's residence and any estates having been transferred to the Church Commissioners. Spiritualities consist of the giving of institution to benefices, the granting of licences for the solemnization of matrimony without the publication of banns (together with the granting of commissions for ordinations *sede vacante* (during a vacancy in the see)). The dean and chapter of the cathedral were until recently the guardians of the spiritualities, but provision has recently been made for the delegation of the diocesan bishop's functions during a vacancy. Thus spiritualities comprise legal aspects of the bishop's authority in oversight or jurisdiction, which is territorially delimited. It seems entirely proper that acknowledgement should be made that this derives from the Crown, the source of all jurisdiction (though not, of course, of the ministerial authority in word and sacrament) in the realm of England.

The involvement of the sovereign is the involvement of a lay person. It is no embarrassment to a church profoundly touched by the Reformation that a lay person should hold large responsibilities in the church. It is simply an outworking of the doctrine of the universal royal priesthood of the baptized. But it also signals symbolically that in the Church of England lay people have major responsibilities and significant privileges. A church that recognizes the spiritual competence of lay persons is likely to be a broad and tolerant church. The laity say the creeds in the context of the liturgy, but (unless they are licensed lay ministers) they are not subject to any other tests of orthodoxy. A church with a lay person as its Supreme Governor cannot be a church dominated by ecclesiastical niceties. As Lord Dacre said in the House of Lords on this point in 1981:

The Church is the congregation of the faithful, clergy and lay alike, and it includes many who loyally adhere without pedantically subscribing. That is the difference between a Church and a sect. An established Church has a particular duty towards the laity: a duty of toleration and comprehension.

(Moyser (ed.), 1985, p. 65)

ESTABLISHMENT AND THE CONSTITUTION

Establishment has wider constitutional implications. It affects more than the Church of England. It is not simply the legal status of the Church of England that is at stake when disestablishment is discussed but the whole fabric of the constitution (for a helpful general discussion, see Bogdanor, 1995). Burke commented that tinkering with the constitution had all the attraction of novelty 'to restless and unstable minds'. But the machinery of a free constitution, he went on, is as intricate and delicate as it is precious (Burke, 1834, pp. 496, 503).

In the (unwritten) British constitution, the Crown is the linchpin of a system of checks and balances (Burke: 'balanced powers'). This constitutional economy gives us a legislature (Parliament) answerable to the electorate, a judicial system largely independent of the executive (the Government), and armed forces that do not owe their ultimate allegiance to politicians. The Crown plays a crucial role in guaranteeing the freedom under the law enjoyed by British citizens. While it is true that European human rights legislation protects the interests of individuals, the constitution provides the structures of political and civil society that facilitate this.

Yet at the same time the Crown is in some sense dependent on the church. The sovereign is seen as answerable to a higher power: crowned and consecrated by the archbishops and bishops of the Church of England, she exercises her office as a duty and privilege that comes from God. Because the monarch is required by the Act of Succession to be in communion with a particular Christian church and is its Supreme Governor, she has not only a constitutional role but also spiritual and moral significance as the guardian of higher civic values (which are only partly dependent on the personal character of the monarch).

Although the special relation of the monarch to the church is confined to the Church of England and does not extend to any other church in the United Kingdom (not even to the established Church of Scotland to the same extent), it is true to say that this relationship underpins the constitution, with its attendant civil liberties, of the United Kingdom as a whole. Thus, in terms of constitutional theory, the role of the monarch vis-à-vis a particular church can be said to be on behalf of or in the service of all persons, communities and institutions that flourish under the constitution. The role of the sovereign is defined in relation to a church that is formally recognized by the state.

It seems understandable that people of republican sentiments should be disestablishmentarians. But people who wish to remain loyal to the institution of the monarchy will be extremely cautious about calling the establishment in question. It has been recognized for centuries that the destinies of the monarchy and the church are bound up together. In our constitutional ecology, the monarchy needs the church just as the polity of the church involves the monarchy. As Habgood has astutely pointed out, disestablishment could leave the monarchy isolated and exposed (Habgood, 1993, p. 148). Hensley Henson said in 1907 that disestablishment would 'strike the Cross from the Crown of the Monarch' (Henson, 1908, p. 18). Bogdanor has pointed out that, were disestablishment to take place, 'the position of the monarchy would be radically affected'. The sovereign would be able to choose any religious faith or none, with the latter possibility leading to a secular monarchy (Bogdanor, 1995, p. 239). In that event, one might ask, what would the constitutional rationale of the monarchy be? As things stand, Crown, church and constitution are bound up together in a delicate constitutional ecology. It is to the benefit of constitution, church and Crown that they should remain so.

Reflecting on the coronation of Queen Elizabeth II in 1953, Shils and Young (1975) commented that the monarchy has its roots in human beliefs and sentiments about the sacred. It is seen as embodying certain moral and civic values that partake of the sacred: generosity, charity, loyalty, justice, respect for authority, individual dignity and personal freedom. The very ordinariness of these values may seem to place them at the opposite pole to the sacred. But this would be a mistaken assumption. They belong to the very substance of the sacred and are widely reverenced as such. (For an account of the sacred aura surrounding the coronation of Elizabeth II, see Pimlott, 1996, pp. 202–14.)

The moral valuation placed upon society derives from the sacredness of its moral values which are held to reflect the nature of that transcendent, superhuman reality that undergirds the world and social life. Under a monarchy, the monarch is the personification of those values (republics have other sacred, uniting symbols, such as the flag, the national anthem, the myth of national destiny, etc.). A once-in-a-lifetime event like a coronation constitutes a ceremonial occasion for affirming those moral and civic virtues by which society lives and without which it knows it would disintegrate. The key to the coronation service is the monarch's solemn promise to abide by the sacred moral principles of society. Shils and Young typify this event in Durkheimian terms as a great national act of communion. People become more aware of their dependence on each other and sense that this is connected with their relationship to the monarch. In affirming the crown they are affirming the values that both bind them together and stand over and above them (Shils, 1975, ch. 8). These coronation vows resonate with all the various sacred vows that are taken in a society: baptism and confirmation vows, marriage vows, those taken by deacons, priests and bishops (and religious), those taken in the direct service of the Crown and those taken on admission into office in any institution. For those who have eyes to see, the self-consecration of the sovereign lends them all strength and support.

The other special ceremonies and celebrations that involve royalty (such as the State Opening of Parliament, Trooping the Colour, the act of remembrance at the Cenotaph, state funerals and the Queen's annual Christmas broadcast) combine the two symbolic discourses of religion and society to promote a sense of national community. Such civic rituals, featuring royalty, dramatize the symbolic community of the nation at the level of the imagination (cf. Thompson in Thomas (ed.), 1988, p. 234). From this symbolic spiritual centre, all communities of faith benefit.

ESTABLISHMENT TODAY

The report on church and state of 1936 was produced when relations between church and Parliament were fraught with tension and recrimination, as a result of the rejection of what became the 1928 Prayer Book, by the House of Commons. The church was insistent on gaining greater spiritual freedom. Yet even that report drew back from advocating disestablishment. It stated:

> The history of Church and nation is, in England, so closely intertwined that the separation could not be effected without injury to both of a kind impossible to forecast and to forestall, which could only be fully appreciated when remedy is out of the question.

The commission set a high price on 'the national recognition of the Christian religion as a power of consecration in its life' and believed that the advantages for the church's mission were incalculable. It pointed out that no one could estimate with any certainty what disestablishment would involve or how far it would go. It recognized that disestablishment, if it were ever to occur, would have to be an act of the state, not of the church: 'The Church cannot disestablish itself.' It wondered what claim the state would make to the finest cathedrals and parish churches and to Westminster Abbey. It warned that, while the possibility of disendowment could not be decisive if disestablishment were thought to be required on grounds of principle, the church would need to count the cost and calculate the effect of disendowment (to which the Church of Ireland and the Church in Wales had been subjected) on its national mission ([Cecil], 1936, pp. 49ff).

In 1933, soon after Parliament had thrown out the revised Book of Common Prayer which had massive support in the counsels of the church and at a time when the Prime Minister had sole discretion in advising the Crown on the appointment of diocesan bishops after simply consulting the Archbishop of Canterbury (see Palmer, 1992), Bishop Hensley Henson was at his most vociferous in condemnation of establishment. Henson had been an ardent advocate of the historic church–state nexus until the Enabling Act of 1919, which he violently opposed. He believed that 'denominational autonomy and national establishment are mutually exclusive' and that the advent of self-government (albeit delegated and limited) for the Church of England gave 'the coup de grâce to the establishment'. He saw this step as substituting the gathered church for the national church (Henson, 1929, pp. 8, 9, 11). His support for establishment was never unconditional (see Chadwick, 1983) and after the crisis between church and Parliament over the revised Prayer Book, Henson, now Bishop of Durham, turned into a formidable advocate of disestablishment.

He compared the establishment of the Church of England to 'a magnificent roof ravaged by the death-watch beetle, yet masking by its splendid appearance a fatal though unheeded weakness' (Henson, 1946, p. 47). Pointing out with brutal frankness the fact that, at that time, establishment meant that the Church of England enjoyed the trappings of privilege without enjoying 'the crown rights of the Redeemer' – freedom to order its spiritual affairs – Henson concluded:

> *Far from ministering to 'spiritual efficiency'* [one of Henson's catch-phrases], *the Establishment now immerses the Church in a bondage to secular forces which is destructive of her true influence, and quite plainly inconsistent with her essential character as a spiritual society, a true and living branch of the Catholic Church which is the Body of Christ.*
>
> (p. 90)

More than sixty years later, with synodical government, control of its doctrine, worship and discipline, and complete responsibility for nominating (if not actually appointing) its bishops, the Church of England has, I believe, nothing to complain about in the conditions of establishment and much to be thankful for. In 1994 the General Synod set its face against reopening the question of establishment and even against reviewing the relation between church and state. Are there any aspects of establishment that can be objected to on principle as contrary to 'the law of Christ' and unacceptable in conscience? The establishment is a given of history, a complex tissue of customary and statutory arrangements deeply embedded in the way society conducts its most serious affairs. Establishment has been profoundly modified and reformed over the past 400 years and will go on evolving. No one particular concrete expression of it is sacrosanct. Any aspect may be looked at again, given the goodwill of Parliament, if it should prove a stumbling block to Christian conscience.

The best approach at this juncture is surely to seize with both hands the pastoral and prophetic opportunities offered by establishment and not to fret about something that few accuse of being harmful and many recognize to be a source of useful service and witness. The Church of England should, therefore, strengthen its relationship to the state by an even more extensive and pervasive involvement in the institutions of the civil society (such as increasing its stake in education, in schools and colleges – a striking example of partnership between church and state, which the Roman Catholic and Methodist Churches also enjoy). At the same time, however, it should look for ways of sharing this partnership more widely with other Christian churches with whom it is in various degrees of unity. In its response to the report of the Wakeham Commission on the reform of the House of Lords it has signalled its willingness to do this.

T. S. Eliot's judgement on establishment, in *The Idea of a Christian Society* (1939), is still worth considering. Setting aside the hypothetical question of whether the legal establishment of a church is desirable in the abstract, Eliot brings the argument down to earth by reminding his readers that we are not being asked whether we want to invent an establishment, but what would be the consequences of dismantling the establishment we have. He draws attention to 'the gravity of the abdication which the Church – whether voluntarily or under pressure – would be making'. Eliot claims that the very act of disestablishing a church separates it more definitely and irrevocably from the life of the nation than if it had never been established in the first place. Altogether, Eliot concludes, disestablishment would amount to the irresponsible creation of an unprecedented condition for English society, the results of which we cannot foresee (Eliot, 1939, pp. 48f).

Criticism of establishment is sometimes offered in terms that are patently anachronistic – 'a misreading of today's situation in response to a belated remorse for yesterday's' (Hastings in Modood (ed.), 1997, pp. 40ff). Establishment is an applied and therefore developing relation between church and state (Carr, 1999). 'Establishment' and 'disestablishment' have become slogans, their meaning detached from their historical origins and constitutional complexities. In a broad sense, establishment stands for the working relationship between the state and a church. Since both are divinely ordained institutions, though historically and sociologically contingent in their expression, it is proper for them to relate to each other. That relationship is a matter of degree: the principle is not at stake. All churches recognize the legitimate role and claims of the state. Almost all welcome some sort of engagement, even amounting to partnership, between church and state for the benefit of both church and society. All operate under the law which protects all citizens from being exploited or coerced. No state is unconcerned about or uninvolved in matters affecting the organized religious life of its citizens. Establishment is not something to be ashamed of, as some would have us believe (see Buchanan, 1994). It represents an entirely proper engagement with and commitment to the God-ordained institution of the state within civil society. The relation between church and state entails mutual obligations and both parties should expect to take the rough with the smooth. Given proper vigilance, establishment can be one of the ways in which the Church exercises its mission in the great community that is the nation.

5

The Lost Language of Church and State

As we move step by step towards an attempt to restate the meaning of a national church for today and the place of establishment in that, and to explore the ecumenical dimension of the national mission of the Church, two things will help us to see the present situation and its possibilities in perspective.

First, we need a grasp of the dominant historical conceptions of the relation between the Church and state in the Bible, the Christian tradition and classical Anglican theology. There are two historical contexts to be considered: that of the non-Christian state that may either tolerate Christianity or persecute it, and that of the Christian state that acknowledges Christianity and may actively support it. We can say straight away that the dominant historical idea of the relation of the Church to the Christian state was that of unity-in-distinction: Church and state were seen as two distinct but coterminous societies within a single national community or commonwealth. (For an account of the relation of Church and state, from the Bible to the Reformation, see Parker, 1955; and for a sophisticated groundwork of political theology, see O'Donovan, 1996.)

Second, we require an understanding of how this latter ideal, in its classical form, was undermined by social, political and ideological pressures. We need to mark the transition to a de facto plural state in the seventeenth century and the subsequent emergence of an ideologically pluralist state in the nineteenth century. Then we need to ask where that leaves us.

THE OLD AND NEW TESTAMENTS

Perhaps the most important contribution of the Old Testament writings to a Christian view of Church and state is the emphasis on divine sovereignty. There are particular and universal aspects to this. God calls Abraham and creates a nation from his descendants (Genesis). He establishes a unique covenantal relation with this nation of Israel, constituting them as a distinct people, with a special calling and destiny (Exodus). In ancient Israel, 'Church' and nation are coterminous. At first, political and religious roles are combined (in Judges and the person of Samuel): they preach, sacrifice and slay. Through prophetic critique of the regime (Elijah and Elisha; Nathan; the eighth-century prophets) the roles of priests and prophets are eventually distinguished from the roles of kings and warriors. But both are servants and ministers of God to the nation/congregation.

In obedience and faithfulness Israel enjoys God's favour and blessing; in disobedience and unfaithfulness she forfeits this and incurs judgement (the canonical prophets and Deuteronomy). The prophets insist that Israel's relation to Yahweh imposes moral, as well as strictly religious, conditions and has consequences for individual behaviour, social justice and their dealings with neighbouring nations.

The radical twist comes with the prophet Amos (but God's concern for other nations and non-Israelites is seen elsewhere, notably in Job and Jonah). Amos takes much that Israel believes is unique to itself and applies it to other nations. If God has a purpose for Israel, he also has a purpose for them. If God punishes them for their evil ways, he will also punish Israel. A parallel is established. Particularity is related to universality. God's sovereignty knows no bounds and his purpose is one of universal blessing, universal justice.

The seeds of the doctrine, found in Romans and in the later Christian tradition, that Church and state are divinely ordained institutions, with complementary roles for human well-being, and both accountable to God for the way that they fulfil them, can be found in the Old Testament. Its literature is also the original source of the belief that particular nations are called, guided and protected by God for a special purpose. This belief has run like a thread through Christian history and there is probably no nation of Christendom that has not embraced it: Catholic and Protestant, Anglican and Puritan, medieval and modern. It is very much alive in Orthodox countries and in the United States today. In Britain it was important through the Second World War and at the time of Queen Elizabeth II's coronation, but has now faded for the time being.

The New Testament writings (see Cullmann, 1957; Pilgrim, 1999) do not contain a single coherent doctrine of the relation of Church and state. Obviously they teach about the nature and mission of the Church. They also recognize the reality of the state – in this case a pagan state – as a separate power to which the Church has to relate. The New Testament's witness on this issue is not monolithic or unambiguous. The element of ambiguity in the New Testament is reflected in the subsequent history and theology of the Church.

In continuity with a strand of conflict between Israel and oppressor nations in the Old Testament and the Apocrypha, there is a fundamental recognition that the claims of God, of the reign or Kingdom of God, have unquestioned priority over the claims of civil government ('Render to Caesar the things that are Caesar's, and to God the things that are God's': Mark 12.17). Christians are to obey God rather than human authority when they clash (Acts 5.29). In the Gospels' presentation of the ministry and teaching of Jesus we find a continual tension, an uneasy coexistence, between the Kingdom of God and secular (pagan) authority. But we find this also in relation to the Jewish authorities (in disputes over the interpretation of Old Testament law and in the cleansing of the Temple). It is as though temporal power is continually in danger of usurping the authority and thwarting the purposes of God.

Given this crucial caveat, however, an attitude of respect and loyalty towards authority is generally inculcated (cf. Romans 13.1; 1 Timothy 2.2; 1 Peter 2.13, 17). This is consistent with the practice in the Jewish Temple and the synagogues of the diaspora. Governors are God's servants and instruments of God's rule, according to Paul in Romans 13. Even when he writes from Roman prisons (in Philippians, Philemon and Colossians), Paul does not call the authority of the Roman state into question or challenge its exercise of justice.

In this dominant strand of the New Testament, Christians are to be model citizens. The imperial authority is to be obeyed. Even when it persecutes the Church, the exemplary behaviour of Christians will confound the opposition. In the post-apostolic age, 1 Clement is, if anything, even more fervent in its positive assessment of the divinely ordained authority of the state and the duty of obedience and loyalty that Christians owe.

It is really only in the Book of Revelation that this basically harmonious vision of the Church dwelling at peace in society and in obedience to civil authority gives way to a dualistic picture of a particular state as the enemy of the Church, as the persecuting Antichrist. Christians will lay down their lives rather than succumb to its idolatrous claims. Nevertheless, the vision persists that ultimately the nations and their kings will walk by the light of God and bring all their glory and honour into the New Jerusalem – thus showing that nations and their rulers have a positive place in the divine economy (Revelation 21.23–6). Among post-apostolic writings, the motif of conflict is echoed in the *Shepherd of Hermas* (mid second century). The sharp critical denunciations of Revelation retain their relevence when the state adopts policies that are profoundly anti-Christian, as with Nazi Germany or the Apartheid regime in South Africa. But active or passive opposition to a particular perverse regime does not invalidate the divine calling of the state to be an agent of God's justice and goodness.

The ambiguity in the New Testament and post-apostolic literature might have been less acute if writers from Paul onwards had been able to distinguish between the institution of the state (ordained by God) and particular regimes that held power (that might be in a state of rebellion against God). Paul's injunctions assume that the state (in the form of a particular regime) is fulfilling its divinely appointed role as it should. It follows that, while the active support of a Christian state should be thankfully attributed to divine providence and the protection of even a non-Christian state is a great good, continual vigilance is laid upon the Church lest the state, under a particular regime, attempt to usurp the obedience that is owed to God.

MEDIEVAL THOUGHT

Constantine's action, in the first quarter of the fourth century, in first tolerating Christianity, then making it the official religion of the empire, created an unprecedented situation for the Church and called for a new departure in political theology. No longer were Christians and churches in a precarious and potentially threatened position in a non-Christian state. The possibility of an active partnership between Church and state had emerged. Constantine now acquired the authority, under Roman public law, to control and direct the Church through its leaders, the bishops, and to take a hand in its doctrine if he were so minded (which he did by calling the Councils of Arles and of Nicaea and by presiding over them) (cf. Ullmann, 1979).

Though the Constantinian establishment of religion, the genesis of Christendom, is sometimes rather glibly pilloried as the paradigm of a false relation between Church and world, we should heed

O'Donovan's point that 'the Christendom idea has to be located correctly as an aspect of the church's understanding of mission' and that, under Christendom, 'the service rendered by the state to the church is to facilitate its mission' (O'Donovan, 1996, pp. 212, 217). He reminds us that 'it was the missionary imperative that compelled the church to take the conversion of the empire seriously and to seize the opportunities it offered'. These were not merely opportunities for power, O'Donovan continues, but for preaching the gospel, baptizing believers, curbing the violence and cruelty of empire and even forgiving former persecutors. Furthermore, 'the same energy drove the church–state dialectic at subsequent moments of transition', whether in the rise of the mendicant orders at the beginning of the second millennium or in the Calvinist reform of ecclesiastical jurisdiction in the sixteenth century. The theological ambiguities of Christendom, of which we are rather one-sidedly conscious today, 'arose from a loss of focus on its missionary context', O'Donovan points out (p. 212).

In medieval political thought (cf. Gierke, 1958), we find the overriding sense of a single community – unity being, as Gierke says (pp. 9f), the ultimate principle of medieval thought. Within this fundamental unity subsisted two inherent powers of jurisdiction, the spiritual and the temporal and these were in a state of precarious balance fraught with rivalry. There is both a universal Church and a universal human community. From Gregory VII (Hildebrand) onwards, that is to say from the second half of the eleventh century, there is a drive to absorb all power into the ecclesiastical hierarchy with the Pope at the apex. He is both a spiritual and a temporal monarch, though he normally delegates temporal jurisdiction to the emperor and under him to princes.

Thus the Church becomes a Christian state in itself and mediates or devolves temporal as well as spiritual authority. Government thereby comes to be seen as an ecclesiastical institution. The movement to absorb all social and political activity and authority within the ambit of the Church reached its term, historically, in the notion, played up by canonists and papal advisers in the fourteenth century, of a global imperial papacy (cf. Ullmann, 1949; Morris, 1989).

The reaction to this hubris, in the conciliar thought of the fourteenth and fifteenth centuries, began to reverse the equation and to seek to bring the Church and its rulers, the popes and bishops, under the authority of temporal rulers with national, territorial concerns in order to reform and unify the Church. Thus the scene is set for the political aspects of the Reformation and the impact of this on the Anglican understanding of the relation of Church and state.

THE REFORMATION TRADITION

The medieval idea of the *corpus christianum* supplies the background to Reformation thought on Church and state also (see further on Luther, Calvin and the English Reformers, Avis, 1982, ch. 9). Pastor and magistrate were both officers of a single Christian society or commonwealth. The new factors in the situation were at the same time theological and political.

In the first place, reform of the Church meant recovering what was regarded as essential and determinative and stripping away whatever was thought to be corrupt accretion. So pastors of the Church were not to wield temporal authority, but to be ministers of word and sacrament. The temporal authority of the pope and his bishops was challenged in Luther's Reformation. The division of labour between Church and state was clarified, with the magistrate having no competence in doctrine, and the clergy resiling from involvement in temporal government. That, at least, is the theory, as Luther and Calvin set it out in their different ways. In England the Lutheran dualism of the Two Kingdoms did not apply, the alliance of Church and state was closer and the roles remained somewhat blurred for a century or two.

In the second place, there inevitably remained a need for temporal authority that would protect and promote the mission of the Church through word and sacrament. Enter the Godly Prince and the doctrine (in England) of the Royal Supremacy. Modelled on Old Testament and Constantinian precedents, the doctrine of the Godly Prince was vital to all forms of the magisterial Reformation. In his sermon at the coronation of Edward VI, Archbishop Cranmer urged the boy-king to be a second Josiah who reformed the Church of God (Israel) in his day (Cranmer, *Remains*, p. 127).

Temporal authority was ordained by God. Its duty was to wield the civil sword to the punishment of wickedness and vice and the protection of good Christian folk in the realm. Part of its reverence for God and responsibility towards God's Church was to protect and promote the mission of the Church. It could do this by providing for and overseeing the outward aspects of the ministry of the pure word of God and the right administration of the sacraments.

This approach was not seen as rendering to Caesar the things of God, because the things of God, according to evangelical theology, were inward and eternal things that could not be shaken by the upheavals of history. Outward and temporal things, that did not impinge on the gospel, were the province of the magistrate. So Melanchthon wrote in the *Apology of the Augsburg Confession*: 'Christ's Kingdom is spiritual; it is the knowledge of God in the heart, the fear of God and faith, the beginning of eternal righteousness and eternal life' (Tappert (ed.), 1959, pp. 222f). Since they are not necessary for salvation, external, temporal matters – even such aspects of the life of the Church as its structures of oversight – are 'things indifferent' *(adiaphora)* and the Church can be content for them to be administered for her by Christian rulers.

The appeal made by the Reformers to the Godly Prince was not a case of the Church invoking the power of the secular state. The state was of course temporal but not secular. It was essentially an appeal from one officer to another within a single community, the Christian commonwealth. 'I perceive no such distinction of the Commonwealth and the Church,' declared Archbishop Whitgift in the reign of Elizabeth I, 'that they should be counted as it were two several bodies governed with divers laws and divers magistrates.' And Whitgift insists again: 'I make no difference between a Christian commonwealth and the Church of Christ' (Whitgift, *Works*, 1.21; 3.312).

If the state was ordained by God and the magistrate was God's agent in caring for the Christian commonwealth, a parallel was set up between Church and state, for the Church also was, of course, divinely ordained and its ministers were God's agents for the welfare of his people. So Cranmer insisted:

> *All Christian princes have committed unto them immediately the whole cure of all their subjects as well concerning the administration of God's word for the cure of souls, as concerning the ministration of things political and civil governance. And in both these ministrations they must have sundry ministers under them … The ministers of God's word under His Majesty be the bishops, parsons, vicars and other such priests as be appointed by His Highness to that ministration … And there is no more promise of God that grace is given in the committing of the ecclesiastical office than it is in the committing of the civil office.*
>
> (Cranmer, *Remains*, p. 116)

So we have in Reformation theology, as in medieval Catholic thought, the idea of parallel but connected divine institutions with parallel but connected divine ministers.

It should not be supposed that this was an Anglican aberration from the purity of Reformation. The connection between Church and state was an operative one in Luther and Calvin too. Both of these Reformers held that the state was divinely ordained and that its agents were, in a sense, God's ministers. Luther's doctrine of the Two Kingdoms did not prevent him appealing to the German nobility to step in and reform the Church in 1520. The close co-operation between church and state – indeed the role of the state in the governance and oversight of the Lutheran *Landeskirchen* in Germany until the First World War – is well known. But perhaps some will suppose that the case of the Reformed tradition is different. Only subtly so.

Calvin begins his treatment 'Of Civil Government' in his *Institutions of the Christian Religion* (1559 edn: Calvin, n.d., vol. 1): 'He who knows how to distinguish between the body and the soul, between the present fleeting life and that which is future and eternal, will have no difficulty in understanding that the spiritual kingdom of Christ and civil government are things very widely separated' (IV, xx, 1). But Calvin immediately states that, though they are distinct, Church and state are 'not adverse to each other'. Civil government is ordained, not merely to nurture justice, peace and stability, but also 'to foster and maintain the external worship of God, to defend sound doctrine and the condition of the Church' (IV, xx, 2). The state is further called to prevent idolatry, blasphemy and offence to religion and to maintain 'a public form of religion' (IV, xx, 3). The officers of the state, the 'magistrates', are 'invested with divine authority' and represent God, on whose behalf they act in the conduct of their duties. The vocation to serve the state is, therefore, 'the most sacred, and by far the most honourable' of all callings and can be regarded as a 'sacred ministry' (IV, xx, 4, 7). Luther and Calvin, just as much as Cranmer, regard the establishment of religion by the Christian state as the norm.

6

The English Anglican Tradition on Church and State

The classical Anglican ideal regarding the relationship between the Christian Church and the state has several components. First, picking up and developing a theme that began to emerge in the Conciliar movement, it affirmed the validity of national expressions of Christianity, on the premise that nationhood was part of God's providential provision for human life. Second, in keeping with the central medieval conception of society, it held to the identity of church and nation in a single community governed by the Christian prince according to the laws of the realm. Third, recovering the balance of earlier medieval thought, it promoted the co-operation of the ecclesiastical and the political spheres in advancing the well-being, both spiritual and temporal, of all citizens. And fourth, it assumed, with all political thought before the Enlightenment, that all societies required a religious foundation. It therefore sought to secure the foundation of the state in the principles of the Christian religion.

RICHARD HOOKER

Richard Hooker's statement of these four elements in his work *Of the Laws of Ecclesiastical Polity* constitutes the theological benchmark on the question of the relation of church and state recognized by later writers, whether Anglican or not and whether they agree with Hooker or not. Though Hooker (1554–1600) gives inherited political and constitutional thought a distinctive turn (see Cargill Thompson, 1972), in major respects Hooker's position was not new but standard. Hooker assumed, like his medieval predecessors from Augustine to Dante and like the Reformers both Continental and English, that church and commonwealth were two facets of a single entity and should co-operate for the spiritual and temporal benefit of citizens and that true religion was the foundation of the state.

To begin with the last point: it was inconceivable to Hooker that a state should not maintain some religion, or should be neutral in religious matters. He assumed that the spiritual care of its citizens was the foremost duty of a state ('pure and unstained religion ought to be the highest of all cares appertaining' to government: Hooker, 1845, vol. 2, pp. 13f: *EP* V, i, 2). This is the pivotal premise on which Hooker builds his theory of the unity of church and state.

In his defence of the Elizabethan settlement of religion, Hooker attacks the dualist theology of the radical Protestants, the proto-presbyterians. They regarded the Church as a distinct community, separate from the state, though existing within it, governed by its own separate officers (elders) and synods. They therefore wanted to exclude even Christian rulers from the governance of the Church. Hooker's patience was sorely tried by this gambit: he accuses them of childishly 'lurk[ing] under shifting ambiguities and equivocations of words in matters of principal weight' (Hooker, 1845, vol. 3: *EP* VIII, i, 2). But Hooker is concerned implicitly throughout his work not only with radical Protestants but also with the Roman Catholic threat to Elizabeth's regime. He has one eye, therefore, to the high medieval papal claims of universal jurisdiction, both spiritual and temporal, including the authority to set up and to cast down temporal rulers – to award and withdraw thrones – and to dictate their principles of policy.

Of course, Hooker acknowledges, a church and a commonwealth are different in nature and are defined differently, but they are not, as the Presbyterians claimed, necessarily made up of different persons. 'The Church of Jesus Christ is every such politic society of men, as doth in religion hold that truth which is proper to Christianity. As a politic society it doth maintain religion; as a church, that religion which God hath revealed by Jesus Christ' (Hooker, 1845, vol. 3, p. 329: *EP* VIII, i, 2). The underlying rationale is strongly christolo-gical, for just as the incarnate Lord Jesus Christ is one person in two natures, divine and human, so a Christian society enjoys a commonality of persons in a distinction of natures: 'They hold the necessity of personal separation, which clean excludeth the power of one man's dealing in both; we of natural, which doth not hinder, but that one and the same person may in both bear a principal sway' (Hooker, 1845, vol. 3: *EP* VIII, i, 2).

The identity of church and society in England could not be more explicitly asserted by Hooker: 'There is not any man of the Church of

England but the same man is also a member of the commonwealth; nor any man a member of the commonwealth which is not also of the Church of England' (Hooker, 1845, vol. 3, p. 330: *EP* VIII, i, 2). Hooker certainly recognizes a difference in the functions of the church and the commonwealth, the one spiritual and heavenly, the other temporal and earthly, but he insists nevertheless that they are 'personally one society'. Spiritual and temporal affairs are merely 'several functions of the same community' (Hooker, 1845, vol. 3, pp. 330ff: *EP* VIII, i, 2–4). This is because the Christian Church is at one and the same time both a 'politic society', existing at the human level, and a 'society supernatural' which holds fellowship with 'God, angels and holy men' (Hooker, 1845, vol. 1, p. 273: *EP* I, xv, 2).

Hooker's legacy to later Anglican theology is thus an ideal of the harmonious co-operation between two God-given functions – spiritual and temporal – of the governance of the one empirical community that is the nation, both functions being united in the person of the Christian prince. The ideal presupposes and rests upon the assumption, unquestioned until modern times, that the state embraces a religious commitment, acknowledges divine revelation and has respect to divine law when formulating its own legislation. The emergence of a plurality of faiths and their inevitable eventual recognition by the state immediately threatens this assumption in its uncompromising form and invites some kind of negotiated adjustment such as successive governments have attempted from Victorian times to the New Labour government of Tony Blair with its stated vision for national moral and spiritual regeneration.

EDMUND BURKE

Two centuries after Hooker, Edmund Burke (1729–97) built his political philosophy on the principle that a nation is a moral entity. 'Mere locality does not constitute a body politic,' states Burke. 'Nation is a moral essence, not a geographical arrangement' (Parkin, 1956, p. 62). Again: 'A nation is not an idea only of local extent and individual momentary aggregation, but it is an idea of continuity, which extends in time as well as in numbers and in space.' The political constitution of the nation, Burke continues, is therefore made 'by the peculiar circumstances, occasions, tempers, dispositions, and moral, civil, and social habitudes of the people, which disclose themselves only in a long space of time' (p. 59). The emphasis on circumstances and occasions reminds us that Burke's method in political philosophy was a sustained attempt to do justice to the utter particularity of human existence – of which the life of a nation was a signal instance. Burke realized, comments Stanlis, that human nature is 'infinitely modified' by such factors as climate, geography, history, religion, nationality and race; by institutions, customs, manners and habits, in fact 'by all the civil circumstances of times, places and occasions' (Stanlis, 1958, pp. 87ff).

Like Hooker, Burke held that the nation, as a moral community, is founded upon religious faith. A human being is by nature 'a religious animal' and the national constitution should reflect this. 'We know, and what is better, we feel inwardly,' wrote Burke in his *Reflections on the Revolution in France*, 'that religion is the basis of civil society, and the source of all good and of all comfort' (Burke, 1910, p. 87). By the establishment of religion in a society by law, the state and its activities are consecrated to a higher purpose (pp. 88f).

For society is a not a merely utilitarian compact of individuals for mundane ends like trade and consumption, but is rather a partnership between all its constituent parts for moral and religious ends too.

> It is to be looked upon with other reverence; because it is not a partnership in things subservient only to the gross animal existence of a temporary and perishable nature. It is a partnership in all science; a partnership in all art; a partnership in every virtue, and in all perfection.

(Burke, 1910, p. 93)

Moreover, the moral and spiritual ends of society require that this partnership is not confined to the present generation. It receives from the past and hands on to the future. Thus 'it becomes a partnership not only between those who are living, but between those who are living, those who are dead, and those who are to be born' (p. 93).

Burke echoes Hooker in taking the logical step from the moral and spiritual foundation of society to the identity of church and commonwealth. 'In a Christian commonwealth the church and the state are one and the same thing: being integral parts of the same whole' (Aston in Aston (ed.), 1997, p. 208: 'Speech on the Petition of the Unitarians', 1792; see also Clark, 1985, pp. 247–58: 'Burke and the Anglican Defence of the State').

Burke upheld the establishment of religion: 'A religious establishment in this state is not contrary to the law of God, or disagreeable to the law of nature, or to the true principles of the Christian religion' (Stanlis, 1958, p. 204). An established church 'consecrated' the state by giving it stability of principles, moral purpose and historical continuity (Stanlis, 1958, p. 227). Burke recognized the interdependence of the church and the Crown, the latter being 'the stay of the mixed constitution' (Stanlis, 1958, p. 228). While Burke was clear that a Christian Church was a national church by its essential nature (Cobban, 1960, p. 93), and believed that the established church and the British constitution stood or fell together, he had a remarkably open and imaginative view of what the establishment of a church might involve.

Burke was an Anglican of the Church of Ireland, though with a Roman Catholic mother and a father who had conformed in order to protect his interests (see O'Brien, 1992). He would allow freedom of worship to dissenters: 'I would have toleration a part of establishment, as a principle favourable to Christianity, and as a part of Christianity' (Aston in Aston (ed.), 1997, pp. 196ff, 189). Burke worked consistently for civil rights for Roman Catholics, but also advocated a broader and more positive form of toleration. The diversity of nations or races contained within the state should be mirrored in a diversity of religious affiliations that are tolerated. And those that are worthy of toleration are also deserving of support: 'All the three religions prevalent ... in various parts of these islands, ought all, in subordination to the legal establishments, as they stand in the several countries, to be all countenanced, protected and cherished' (Stanlis, 1958, p. 227). Burke argued that the terms of the Protestant ascendancy, secured by the Revolution of 1688, including the coronation oath, did not preclude civil liberties, including some kind of state recognition, being extended to non-Anglicans (see O'Brien, pp. 477f).

Church and state, for Burke, are twin bodies that need each other. In their social function, they are related, in his thought, as morals are to laws. While the state maintains the national laws and the formal structure of society, the Church fosters the more local and intimate sphere of morals or mores (what Burke calls 'manners'). This is the realm of the inner spirit of human life, the mental habit and temper of a people built up over many centuries, the essential fabric of relationships and communities. But Burke was quite clear which of these two social agencies was the more important (Stanlis, 1958, p. 223).

Altogether Burke perpetuates the Hookerian ideal of the unity of church and state on the basis of an acknowledged moral and spiritual purpose for society. While committed to the constitutional principles of 1688, with its guaranteed Protestant ascendancy, Burke antici-pated nineteenth-century developments by arguing that state recognition and support of religious societies other than the Church of England were no threat to the established status of Anglicanism in England. His understanding of establishment was flexible and generous.

SAMUEL TAYLOR COLERIDGE

The last work that Coleridge (1772–1834) published during his lifetime, *On the Constitution of the Church and State* (1830), proved to be one of the most seminal of discussions of this topic. The relation between church and state had preoccupied Coleridge all his life. His father, who was both parish priest and schoolmaster at Ottery St Mary, Devon, symbolized the connection. Hazlitt tells us in his essay 'My First Acquaintance with Poets' that Coleridge, then a young Unitarian minister, seemed like a vision of Christ or John the Baptist when he preached 'upon peace and war; upon church and state – not their alliance, but their separation – on the spirit of the world and the spirit of Christianity, not as the same, but as opposed to one another' (Hazlitt, 1927, p. 22).

In later life, however, Coleridge was a bulwark of the established Church of England, trinitarian in his beliefs and his theological method, orthodox in his theology, deeply read in seventeenth-century divinity and a champion of Luther and the Reformation (for the latter see Avis, 1989, pp. 239-44). Coleridge believed the Church of England to be 'apostolic in its faith, primitive in its ceremonies, unequalled in its liturgical forms'. It had nurtured 'more bright and burning lights of genius and learning than all other Protestant churches since the Reformation' (Coleridge, 1912, p. 606).

Coleridge's work on church and state was called forth by fears about imminent Roman Catholic emancipation. In this work he distinguishes (though not very clearly, it must be said) between: first, the Church of Christ, the Church catholic; second, the national church (in an idiosyncratic sense for which Coleridge coined the term 'clerisy'); and finally, the Church of England, the union of the

Church of Christ and the national church or clerisy through a 'blessed accident' of history.

The Church of Christ could not be brought into conjunction with the state, but only with the world. By the same token it could not be brought into antithesis to the state, but only to the world. Though a catholic and apostolic church exists *in* England, it is not the same as the 'constitutional and ancestral Church *of* England' (Coleridge, 1976, pp. 117, 125).

The national church, the 'true Church *of* England' or 'Clerisy of the nation', is greater than the Church of England by law established (p.125). It comprises the learned of all denominations, the practitioners of all the liberal arts and sciences, all who contribute to the 'cultivation' or true civilization of the realm (p. 46). Coleridge insists that the national church or clerisy is still 'an estate of the realm', counterbalancing the landed interest, on the one hand, and the manufacturing and trading classes, on the other (p. 77). He foresees with foreboding the emergence of a pluralist and therefore secular state, in which the national church will no longer be 'a great venerable estate of the realm' as in the supposedly 'dark age' of Queen Elizabeth, the so-called 'unenlightened times' of Burleigh, Hooker, Spenser, Shakespeare and Bacon! The clerisy will become merely one of many sects, churches or communities, distinguished from the others by having its priesthood (so to speak) – largely the Anglican clergy – endowed by the parliament of the day (p. 61).

In his *Table Talk* Coleridge claimed that 'the National Church requires, and is required by, the Christian Church, for the perfection of each'. For if there were no national church (or clerisy), the merely spiritual church would tend to become an ecclesiastical tyranny, like the papacy, or else would disintegrate into a multiplicity of fanatical sects, as in seventeenth-century England. He further believed that liberty of conscience could only be guaranteed where there was an established, national church, distinct from the spiritual Church of Christ (J. R. Barth, 1969, p. 168). The national church, for Coleridge – though not exactly identical with the Church of England – acts as a sort of buffer zone, both connecting and keeping separate the temporal interests of the state and the spiritual interests of Christ's Church.

Coleridge bears witness to the responsibility of a national church to all members of the community, with the emphasis on their moral and intellectual education, and points, albeit idiosyncratically, towards the ecumenical vision of a united national church.

WILLIAM EWART GLADSTONE

The last great vindication of the Hookerian ideal of the identity of church and state – its swan song, in fact – was made in 1838 by Gladstone (1809–98) in *The State in Its Relation with the Church*. Gladstone had read and annotated Coleridge's *Church and State*, finding it 'alike beautiful and profound'. He was indebted to Coleridge's notion of the clerisy and attracted to Coleridge's method of first setting forth a transcendent *idea*, attained by deductive reasoning combined with insight into human nature, and then asking what steps were necessary in order to realize this idea. (He found Coleridge deficient in such concrete details.) Gladstone's own treatise of 1838 on state and church 'relies strongly on Hooker for its approach to the Church, but on Burke and Coleridge for the State' (Matthew, 1997, p. 62; see his whole illuminating discussion, pp. 36–43, 63–5).

Gladstone's sense that, while the apostolicity of the Church always gives it its primary identity, national history and other contingent factors modify the essence of the Christian Church into distinctive, diverse modes of existence with local traditions and practices, vindicates his standing as an authentic interpreter of Anglicanism. On this score he stands with Hooker, Burke and Coleridge and moves somewhat apart from Newman and the Tractarians. Because it is 'the vivifying and ennobling principle of all national life', the national religion reflects the innate characteristics of the nation it serves. Gladstone's acceptance of 'national religion' made Thomas Arnold see him as an ally (Matthew, 1997, pp. 63f).

For Gladstone, the nation was to be viewed not according to Utilitarian, Enlightenment assumptions as a conglomeration of individuals, but on Platonic, Coleridgean, idealist principles, as a single unified person, an organic whole, whose ultimate ends are moral and therefore spiritual. Gladstone praised Hooker's theory because it involved 'the great doctrine that the state is a person, having a conscience, cognisant of matter of religion, and bound by all constitutional and natural means to advance it' (Gladstone, 1841, vol. 1, p. 14). The state and the family are the principle constitutive moral communities. Of the state Gladstone claims:

> It is the office of the state in its personality to evolve the social life of a
> man, which social life is essentially moral in the ends it contemplates,

in the subject matter on which it feeds, and in the restraints and motives it requires; and which can only be effectually moral when it is religious.

(Gladstone, 1841, vol. 1, p. 93)

The assumption that the state is a moral personality implies that the state must make moral choices and that these choices are to be grounded in a unified body of truths, or at least that nearest approximation to that. What is certain, as far as Gladstone is concerned, is that 'it cannot at all consist with jointly embracing systems that are fundamentally or substantially at variance'. In other words, the moral nature of the state is incompatible with religious pluralism (Gladstone, 1841, vol. 1, pp. 93, 125f).

An established, national, monopolistic church is interested in (Gladstone here ironically adapts Jeremy Bentham's famous slogan of Utilitarianism) 'the greatest holiness of the greatest number', that is to say, the largest quantity of real and genuine religion in the population (Gladstone, 1841, vol. 1, pp. 258ff). But a religion established by law is not interested merely in a spiritual élite, but in those who are struggling to maintain their faith, the wistful half-believers, the backsliders, and those of little faith. An established religion did not have to strive to assert itself; it was therefore likely to be 'more calm, more catholic, less alloyed by the contagion of spiritual pride and selfishness' (vol. 1, pp. 259, 261). Gladstone wanted a church that, as well as embracing the devout and committed, would be hospitable to

those who are too timid to make religious profession; those who hesitate between this world and he next; those who give a limited and insufficient scope to the action of Christian principle; those who attend Christian ordinances only in compliance with human opinion; and those who see nothing in Christianity but a system of outward forms, in an establishment nothing but a method of preserving social order and of repressing religious extravagance.

(vol. 1, p. 259)

Gladstone later confessed that his attempt to revive the Hookerian ideal of the unity of church and commonwealth was impracticable even before it appeared. Gladstone himself had supported Roman Catholic emancipation in 1829 – though, as a Tory at the time, he felt obliged to resign his ministerial office (see Butler, 1982). By the time Gladstone wrote his treatise, England was already (as we shall see in the next section) a religiously plural and pluralist state. The Hookerian model had never been entirely true to the facts and had become progressively less so since the time it was articulated. Although Gladstone confessed that his ideal was doomed, he never disowned it, nor did he substitute another: he merely reluctantly conceded that it was no longer practicable (cf. Vidler, 1945, p. 25; Vidler's discussion still repays attention).

Gladstone's rearguard action was flawed by internal tensions. As Macaulay perceptively argued in his celebrated attack in the *Edinburgh Review* (Macaulay, 1905), Gladstone had developed a major premise, that of the organic state with a national moral conscience, to support his minor premise, that of the confessional, monopolistic Anglican Church. The implications of the major premise are not so much worked out as asserted in a global fashion over against the reductionist approach of the Utilitarians. (Macaulay frankly admitted: 'We consider the primary end of government as a purely temporal end, the protection of the persons and the property of men': Macaulay, 1905, p. 497.) However, as Matthew suggests, when Gladstone came to consider the civil rights of dissenting individuals, whose freedom from persecution had been protected by modifications to the Anglican establishment over a century and a half, he was 'forced back upon the utilitarian tradition which he had earlier in the book so vehemently condemned'. Matthew concludes:

> *Thus at the heart of the book lay a profound contradiction, the result of the attempt to use quite separate philosophical traditions to justify first an Ideal of society, then practical anomalies to that ideal which already existed. There was, therefore, a lifeline to utilitarianism and consequently pluralism when the ship sank.*

(Matthew, 1997, p. 63)

THOMAS ARNOLD

Meanwhile, Thomas Arnold (1795–1842) had set out a vision of a national church that took religious diversity seriously and attempted to heal the wounds created by the Act of Uniformity of 1662 and the consequent exclusion of Dissenters from the national church. In his cryptic work *Principles of Church Reform* (published in 1833 – the same year that the *Tracts for the Times* began to appear), Arnold argued in Hookerian and Burkean mode that the state had inescapable moral and spiritual functions. He deplored 'the false and degrading notions of civil society' that had prevailed in the Enlightenment with its fostering of rationalistic individualism. Society had been regarded, he claimed, as a collection of separate individuals, each looking to his own interest. The state had been viewed as a sort of policeman whose job was to prevent competing individuals from destroying each other (Arnold, 1845, p. 265). But with Hooker, Burke and Coleridge, Arnold affirmed that the state, the only power sovereign over human life in this world, has proper moral and spiritual ends and is concerned for the intellectual and moral happiness of its subjects. The state is like a teacher who aims at the complete well-being of his pupil (Arnold, 1874, p. 38).

The moral and spiritual ends of society can only be served by a truly national church whose basis of unity is found in a shared way of life and a common moral purpose. Action, rather than belief, is the bond of unity (according to Arnold) in all societies, whether states or churches. These institutions aim at goodness before truth. Action is at the behest of the will but belief is spontaneous and not at our command: 'We may consent to act together, but we cannot consent to believe together ... action being a thing in our own power.' Therefore, Arnold continues, 'the social bond cannot directly require for its perfection more than union of action' (Arnold, 1874, pp. 39f).

Like Burke, Arnold found the ground of unity in a common tradition, a common practice. The ideal of a church broadly coextensive with the nation had been abandoned in 1662 and 1689, but in these better and happier times could now be once again accomplished (Arnold, 1874, p. 248). Dissenters could be included because a national church did not mean a uniform church. A national church, Arnold argued elsewhere, could include 'persons using different ritual and subscribing different articles' (Stanley, 1891, p. 431).

On the basis of accepted diversity, church and state could be reunited. If the state has religious and moral purposes, its governors may become governors of the church. This obviates the need in the church for sacerdotal hierarchy (Arnold's *bête noire* and the great sin of which he accused the Tractarians). When church and state are separated, the state becomes worldly and profane, the church becomes 'formal, superstitious and idolatrous'. The church is truly the soul of the state; the state is the body of the church. In the final analysis, the perfect state and the perfect church are 'identical' (Arnold, 1874, pp. 50ff: reply to Macaulay's review of Gladstone).

The strengths of Thomas Arnold's theory are its emphases on practice and diversity. The convergence between the churches in their liturgical practice and the emergence of forms of ecumenical co-operation and patterns of oversight, in the last two decades of the twentieth century, suggest that common practice implies theological common ground that springs back into recalcitrant oppositions only when we attempt to abstract it from concrete practice and articulate it in divergent theological languages. This irreducible ecumenical diversity is mirrored also in the internal diversity of the major Christian churches. They already embrace diversity of worship and belief. A united church need be no more uniform than its con-tributory traditions. The combination of practice and diversity lends itself to the notion of a national church that is marked by concrete involvement in the local community and reflects the rich variety of regional cultures within a national community.

FREDERICK DENISON MAURICE

F. D. Maurice (1805–72) was a great believer in 'facing the facts', including the facts of abiding spiritual realities in the midst of social changes. He had felt the impact of Protestant dissent in a childhood spent among Quakers and Unitarians. In *The Kingdom of Christ* (1838, 2nd edn 1842) Maurice battled against all forms of sectarian-ism (as he saw it), which for him included Roman Catholicism in England. He argued for a moral unity of church and state as a witness to and partial embodiment of 'the divine order' of the Kingdom of Christ. Subtitled 'Hints to a Quaker Respecting the Principles, Constitution and Ordinances of the Catholic Church', the work claimed that the Quakers, with their misplaced non-sacramental spirituality and their rejection of national distinctions, failed to achieve a universality or catholicity of spiritual existence themselves (Maurice, 1958, vol. 1, pp. 60, 64).

In contrast, Maurice points out, the sixteenth-century Reformers accepted the principle of the distinctive character and calling of nations. Imbued with the Old Testament, they well knew that God's plan of salvation had taken the form of his dealings with a particular nation (Maurice, 1958, vol. 1, pp. 77, 80). Nations, like families, point to a spiritual order in the world. The Jewish nation had, in fact, sprung from one elect family. Nation and family are subordinate parts of that spiritual constitution of the world – 'the divine order' – of which the Christian Church is the fullest manifestation (Maurice, 1958, vol. 2, pp. 231ff, 239f; F. Maurice, 1884, vol. 1, p. 306).

For Maurice, the state is just as much a divine creation as the church. In the providence of God, church and state are mutually implicated in a relation that is unity but not complete identity. Each retains the critical distance to correct the shortcomings of the other. In reply to the sectarian separatist, who fears that the church may become secularized by contact with the state, Maurice insists that both church and state do not need help from each other in order to fall into secularization (Maurice, 1958, vol. 2, pp. 240ff; cf. pp. 305ff). The relation between church and state is, Maurice states, 'a union which has cemented itself by no human contrivances, and which exists in the very nature of things' (p. 312).

Thirty years later, Maurice glosses the union of church and state as 'the cooperation of spirit with law'. Both are needed and complement each other. The state is not what churchmen and statesmen of various schools of thought have declared it to be: 'a vulgar earthly institution, which might do the dirty work of the Church, paying its ministers, persecuting its foes, or determining its teachings'. It is rather 'a sacred and divine institution bearing a witness for law and justice' (F. Maurice, 1884, vol. 2, pp. 585ff).

'Claim your position in Christ!' is the heart of Maurice's message. The Church of England tells all its children that 'they have no less right to claim their places in her as members of Christ than they have to claim their places in the nation as subjects of the Queen', or, for that matter, as members of a human family (F. Maurice, 1884, vol. 2, p. 376). The eschatological unity of humanity under the headship of the incarnate Jesus Christ is the foundation for a universal human community. Anglicanism's expression of this (which is at the same time an anticipation of its fulfilment) in the form of its pastoral inclusiveness and weddedness to the community at all levels, was the source of its attraction for Maurice.

The theological undergirding of F. D. Maurice's view of the relation of church and society, church and state, is christological and eschatological. Jesus Christ is Lord. He is the Head of humanity. As the Greek Fathers taught, he recapitulates humanity in himself. There is a latent union with Christ that can be postulated of every person. This is presupposed in baptism. It simply needs to be claimed, owned and lived. In the Church the latent becomes the patent. The pastoral mission of the Church is pursued with patience and confidence, in the knowledge that what Christ has brought about through his incarnation, death and resurrection is a reality 'out there' just waiting to be realized. In this spirit of expectation the Church can trust itself to other socio-political structures, knowing that they too are God-given and play their part in witnessing to and manifesting the divine order.

MANDELL CREIGHTON

Though he flourished in the last quarter of the nineteenth century, Mandell Creighton (1843–1901) provides what is perhaps the last uncompromising statement of the Hookerian ideal. (Hensley Henson would be another example, but he turned from being the most formidable advocate of establishment to being its most formidable critic.) So although Mandell Creighton postdates the crucial developments of the first half of the nineteenth century, beginning with the Whig reforms of the late 1820s and early 1830s which ushered in the pluralist state, he may be taken as the last representative of the classical Anglican ideal. (For an introduction to Creighton and his thought, see Fallows, 1964, esp. ch. 5: 'The Church and the Nation'.)

Creighton believed passionately in the principle of a national expression of the Christian religion. In his essay of 1896 'The Idea of a National Church', Creighton argued that, though the Church of Christ is a new creation and belongs to the spiritual order, it has its home on earth in the natural order 'by which it is constantly limited, and from which it cannot be completely disentangled'. The differentiation of nations is part of God's providential purpose. Their diversity mirrors the diversity of created species. The legitimacy of diverse national expressions of Christianity 'simply recognises the facts of human history' (Creighton, 1901, pp. 207f, 210f, 213).

Creighton was, not surprisingly, therefore, a staunch defender of the Church of England as the national church. National churches were not opposed to the character of the Church of Christ, affirmed in the creed, as one, holy, catholic and apostolic, because these attributes receive variegated expression in contingent historical circumstances. 'The Church of Christ is one, in the same way as mankind is one.' The unity is primary, the diversity secondary.

National churches have, as the Thirty-Nine Articles state, authority in rites, ceremonies and discipline, but not over the creeds (Creighton, 1901, pp. 212, 207). Creighton believed that Anglicanism shared with the Eastern Orthodox Churches the principle that a church can be both national and catholic (L. Creighton, 1904, vol. 2, p. 443).

Creighton was therefore committed to the principle of the co-operation of church and state in the interests of the one commonwealth of citizens. He defined the state as 'the community which is concerned with the arrangements of the common life' and the church as 'the community concerned with setting forth the principles on which all life rests'. Therefore, he asked, why should not church and state exist side by side, in a state of complementarity and harmony. 'Church and state are not contradictory things'; they are precisely 'the nation looked at from different points of view'. As a national church, the Church of England stands in 'an organic relation to the national life of the country' (L. Creighton, 1904, vol. 2, pp. 98, 384, 443).

Creighton's assumption was, of course, the Burkean one that the common life, with which the state was concerned, was not a purely mundane, material affair, but was of a moral and spiritual nature. The disestablishment of the Church of England, if that were ever to happen, would be a major blow, not only to England but to Europe, because it would mean the abandonment of an ancient, historical connection between the nation and the Christian religion. 'A national church means a national recognition of the supreme law of God.' The rupture would damage the state more than the church (L. Creighton, 1904, vol. 2, pp. 99, 384). For the nation to 'deliberately repudiate any organic connexion between the basis of its national life and the profession of the Christian faith' seemed to Creighton 'a calamity which could never be repaired' (Creighton, 1901, p. 31).

RECOVERING THE LOST LANGUAGE OF CHURCH
AND STATE

As we have briefly traced the tradition through biblical, medieval, Reformation and Anglican thought, several central teachings have emerged. They are unfashionable today. The liberal relativism that pervades the public policy of most churches has sapped our confidence. There seems to be a loss of nerve to make bold and distinctive claims on behalf of the Christian revelation. Like so much of the Christian tradition, the Church's language of church and state has been well and truly forgotten. It sounds strange even to Christian ears. But it is not the less valid for that. To recover, re-interpret and re-affirm this sort of language is not an exercise in nostalgia. It can be detached from the setting of, say, Hooker's England which has long since passed away. The convictions that, I believe, the tradition enshrines can be summarized in the following theses:

- The institution of the state is ordained by God as a creation ordinance for the well-being of humanity. Like the Church, the State is a divine institution. The State should be distinguished from the government. Particular political regimes are not, of course, so ordained. Just as the structures of the Church can fail and become corrupt, so that it needs reformation and renewal, so too the powers of the State can be perverted by evil or misguided regimes. As the enduring structure of governance, embodying in various different models principles of vocation, responsibility, representation and accountability, the State should be honoured, served and defended. We should interest ourselves in the constitutional, legal foundation of the State under which, or within which, we live. The truth that the role of the State is willed by God needs to be re-affirmed today in view of the widespread distrust and apathy with regard to national, regional and local government.
- Those who serve the State, like those who serve the Church, are doing God's good work. Like the sacred ministry of the Church, the service of the State remains God's work even when carried out in an inadequate or unworthy manner or for the wrong motives. There is a Christian calling to serve the community in a representative way through the structures of governance that comprise the State. The fact that the comparison that earlier writers made, between the ordained ministry of word and sacrament and the ministry of governance in the State, seems far-fetched today is a measure of how far church and society have drifted from their moorings in the Christian tradition. However, the principle that those who offer themselves in the service of the State are serving God's good purposes remains true. I do not think I have ever heard that said by church leaders at the time of a General Election, yet it helps to explain why we believe we should expect a high standard of personal conduct and of professional accountability in our elected politicians.

- Every society needs a foundation in transcendent truths and values. A merely instrumental justification for the State is inadequate. It does not simply exist to provide for the material or even cultural needs of its people. The State is a corporate moral person. It has moral responsibilities and is morally accountable in the persons of its representatives. Politicians are its servants. They therefore have an obligation to serve the ends and uphold the values that are intrinsic to the State. The liberal relativism that holds that people should be free to live as they please provided that they do not thereby inflict harm on others cannot sustain a coherent society. In order to flourish, a society needs to commit itself publicly to certain goals – goals that are inevitably long term – and values that transcend individual fulfilment and selfish gratification. These include: compassionate care for the less fortunate, a sense of moral obligation to others and to the community, the privileging of the primary, irreducible relationships of marriage and parenthood, stable family life, the values of self-discipline and restraint, the wider relationships of belonging and serving that build up a community – all values that the Christian faith promotes.

- If that is basically true, a secular state is a contradiction in terms. A state cannot be without ultimate concerns and commitments. When earlier divines stated that every state upholds a certain religion, even if not the Christian one, that was not merely a sociological observation. A set of beliefs that evoke the transcendent and a set of values that look beyond the individual and the present electoral term are essential for a healthy society. The Christian Church, for all its failings, offers precisely these beliefs and values on the basis of divine revelation and can therefore speak with conviction and without apology. I am convinced that there are millions of people in our nation today who long for the Church to speak these truths clearly and boldly. Though such a move would generate opposition from some, it would also evoke respect and gratitude from many others.

- As twin divinely ordained institutions – two channels through which God works for the well-being of God's human creatures – church and state must necessarily relate to each other. They cannot ignore each other's existence. This can be put more positively by saying that they have mutual obligations and must, therefore, reach an arrangement that respects the calling and integrity of the other. The Church should not attempt to usurp the role of the State, legislating for the temporal aspects of society. The State should not attempt to dominate or control the Church or to usurp its spiritual authority. But that cannot mean that there is no interaction between them. In cognisance of its moral and spiritual obligations, the State may give formal recognition, in law and in the constitution, to the Christian religion and to one or more particular churches. This acknowledgement provides the Church with pastoral and prophetic opportunities that it cannot renounce without betraying its mission. It is helped to bring its ministry to bear on the life of the nation at every level: in local communities; in the numerous institutions that make up civil society; and nationally, in terms of public doctrine. It will not always be heeded, but to speak and sometimes to be ignored is better than to be structurally marginalized and socially invisible.

- The state dimension of the Church's mission is related to its other dimensions. The territorial pastoral ministry in all the many local communities and the sector ministries to institutions undergird and validate the message that the Church seeks to put across at the national level. The local, the institutional and the national dimensions of the Church's mission interlock. An effective mission in terms of civil society will be tenuous in the absence of an active relationship with the State. The territorial ministry of the priest in the parish and of the bishop in the diocese depend on the conditions of establishment in law – though this seems not to be realized by those bishops and clergy who blithely give credence to disestablishmentarian ideas.

- This combination of state recognition and territorial/institutional ministry – colloquially referred to as 'establishment' – takes many forms and undergoes continual modification and negotiation. It is not in principle incompatible with a plural society where the role of other faith communities is also acknowledged in law and in practice. This is not purely a modern issue, but has been around for centuries. As we shall see, a sophisticated model, combining tolerance of diverse faith communities and affirmation of one in particular for the benefit of all, is attainable, provided that one itself supports the values of tolerance, dialogue and hospitality.

7

Church, State and Modern Pluralism

The emergence of a plural society goes back as far as the sixteenth century. Hooker's *Of the Laws of Ecclesiastical Polity* presupposes the unity of church and nation. They were one commonwealth with spiritual and temporal aspects. But even when Hooker wrote his treatise there were already two groups in society who were outside the church–state nexus: the radical Protestant Separatists, offshoots of the Anabaptists, who rejected the idea of a Christian state on the imperial, Constantinian model, and the recusant Roman Catholics whose first loyalty was to the pope who claimed to have deposed Elizabeth from the throne and designated her heretic and outlaw. Both these groups opposed the unity of church and nation at risk of their lives.

By the mid seventeenth century the descendants of the Separatists, the Independents, would exert a decisive influence in the Civil War period and shortly afterwards the Roman Catholics would gain control of the throne – covertly in the case of Charles II and overtly in the case of James II. In the Toleration Act of 1689, the state recognized the validity of corporate dissent from the national church. As Norman Sykes reiterated in his evidence to the 1935 commission on church and state, since that date the continuance of establishment has been 'an act of grace, not of right' ([Cecil], 1936, pp. 287, 300). By the end of the seventeenth century, those outside the church which was the spiritual arm of the state included Baptists, Presbyterians, Quakers, Roman Catholics and the Non-Jurors (who rejected the transference of the throne by Act of Parliament from James II to William of Orange).

By the Act of Union with Scotland in 1707, an established Presbyterian Church came under the jurisdiction of the parliament in Westminster, with Presbyterians taking their place there. The sovereign was pledged to 'maintain and preserve inviolably' both the Scottish and English churches (Bogdanor, 1995, pp. 215f). The repeal of the Test and Corporation Acts in 1828 abolished the barriers against Roman Catholics and Protestant Dissenters holding civil office. (For a useful account of the Whig legislation of the 1820s, see Varley, 1992, ch. 5.) Similarly, the Act of Union with Ireland in 1800–1 made Parliament responsible for 5.5 million Roman Catholics – equal to more than a third of the population of England and Wales (Chadwick, 1987, 1, pp. 8f). When Roman Catholic Emancipation inevitably followed in 1829, there were fears for the safety of the Church of England as a result of Irish Roman Catholic Members taking their places in Parliament (Chadwick, 1987, 1, pp. 1–24). Bishop Van Mildert of Durham opposed Roman Catholic Emancipation on the grounds that Roman Catholics owed their primary allegiance to a temporal ruler who was beyond the jurisdiction of the British sovereign state. At least Scottish Presbyterians were no threat to the Protestant constitution, secured at the Revolution of 1688! But now a Roman Catholic could be the sovereign's first minister – though it was inconceivable that he could advise the Crown on the appointment of bishops in the established church. Roman Catholic Emancipation marked symbolically the end of the old legislative order. But even more than Roman Catholic Emancipation, it was the re-establishment of the Roman Catholic hierarchy in 1850 – the so-called 'papal aggression' – with the provocative location of the Archdiocese at Westminster, that brought home to Anglicans the fact that the state no longer controlled and protected the Anglican religion in England and Wales (Hastings, 1991, p. 27).

Jews were eventually admitted to Parliament in 1858, being permitted to swear on the Old Testament (Chadwick, 1987, 1, pp. 484ff), and by 1886 atheists were no longer excluded. The general election of 1906 (the Liberal landslide) was the first to result in a House of Commons that was not predominantly Anglican. In 1916 the Liberal Lloyd George became the first non-Anglican and Free Church Prime Minister (those of his predecessors who were by baptism Scots Presbyterians having practised Anglicanism in

England). Now what price the House of Commons as the lay synod of the Church of England?

The various civil registration acts further eroded the Anglican monopoly of spiritual welfare. Before the Civil Registration Act of 1837 a baptism certificate functioned as a birth certificate. Now the legal sanction for baptism was removed and that had a catastrophic effect on the numbers of baptisms in some parts of the country. The Civil Registration Acts 'were a crucial factor in the Anglican adjustment from national Church to denomination'. The disgrace of overcrowded and neglected churchyards was tackled by the Public Health Act of 1848 and the Cemetery Acts of 1852–53 which severed one more link in the identity of church and community, the parish churchyard (Knight, 1995, pp. 25, 88, 103ff). Lord Hardwicke's Marriage Act of 1753 regularized the solemnization of matrimony and brought it under the control of the Anglican clergy, but paradoxically Quakers and Jews were permitted to conduct their own weddings (this was confirmed by the acts of 1836–37).

A further paradox is the fact that as the Church of England spread alongside the British Empire throughout the globe, the Anglican monopoly was undermined, not only by the presence of other Christian churches, but also by the existence of other faiths. How was this compatible with the sovereign's spiritual jurisdiction over the realm? By the nineteenth century, the Act of Supremacy of Elizabeth I seems to have been interpreted as applying not so much geographically and territorially, as personally and individually, to members of the Church of England within a given territory (Hinchcliff, 1997). As Hastings comments, the Empire signalled the end of Erastianism, of state control of the church, because the Empire could only function politically by accepting religious pluralism (Hastings, 1991, p. 25). So today the Queen is Head of State for peoples of many faiths, whose prayers she has consistently requested throughout her reign, but Supreme Governor only of the Church of England.

The disestablishment and disendowment of the Church of Ireland in 1869 and of the Church in Wales in 1921 showed that Parliament would not balk at drastic action where the national interest or public opinion seemed to require it. Charles Gore was one of the very few bishops of the Church of England to support Welsh disestablishment. In a speech in the House of Lords in 1913 he said:

> *To claim to be the Established Church, to claim to retain that position in face of the refusal of the great majority of the inhabitants to concede*

that demand, is to claim an immoral position. It is a position that is demoralizing to religion.

Gore went on to doubt whether establishment could long survive in England, though it seemed secure in Scotland (Nicholls (ed.), 1967, p. 195). In actual fact, the establishment of the Church of England has proved resilient and durable because both church and state have been comparatively sensitive to the need to adapt to changing social conditions and patterns of religious practice.

These interventions were taken at the time – and still remain – as a warning to the Church of England. Just as being disestablished is no protection against state intervention (as the history of the Scottish churches in the mid nineteenth century shows), so the fact of establishment brings no state guarantees.

How did these profound legislative changes in the nineteenth century affect the idea of a union of church and state? How did establishment look by the beginning of the twentieth century? In her account of the parliamentary reform of the Church of England in the first half of the nineteenth century, Olive Brose concluded that by the mid 1840s 'the attempt to assert the Church's national function had lost any connection with reality' (Brose, 1959, p. 209). Van Mildert believed, at the time of the Whig reforms, that the principle of pluralism threatened 'the existence of any religious Establishment whatsoever' (Varley, 1992, p. 140). It seemed to the moderate Tractarian W. F. Hook in 1846 that the Church of England existed simply as 'one of the great corporations of the country, claiming from the state, like every other corporation, protection for its rights and its property' (Varley, 1992, p. 140). When Bishop Blomfield knew that Catholic Emancipation would go through, he asked in consternation, in the Lords, 'Where will be the Establishment?' Hensley Henson commented in his journal in 1919, on the smooth passage of the Enabling Act through Parliament, that the establishment 'had fallen like an over-ripe fruit' (Henson, 1929, p. 8).

J. N. Figgis, normally the most acute Anglican interpreter of the place of the Church of England in the modern state, insisted that by the beginning of the twentieth century, all talk about the national church was misleading and dangerous (Nicholls, 1975, pp. 103f). But this judgement needs to be scrutinized carefully. Against a background of establishment privilege, Figgis advocated (endorsing an earlier slogan) 'a free church in a free state' (see Figgis, 1913). However, before endorsing that formula ourselves, in our very different current circumstances of the erosion of privilege and hierarchy, on the one hand, and the virtual self-government of the Church of England, on the other, we should ask two questions about each half of Figgis' equation. In what sense is it right for the Church of Christ to be 'free'? Is it not to be committed to service in civil society? And is the idea of a state free of all religious commitments – a secular constitution – really an attractive one?

ESTABLISHMENT AND OTHER COMMUNITIES OF FAITH

The new dimension in the debate on establishment is, of course, the presence of other faith communities, the aspirations and claims that they might make to some kind of national recognition. Bradney has shown (though he is sometimes tendentious) that adherents of other faiths are sometimes disadvantaged by English law which can cause them practical difficulties (Bradney, 1993). There is not yet a 'level playing field' in law or public life between faiths. However, the question of the place of non-Christian religions in national life is not our immediate concern here, since we are pursuing the vision of the mission of a united national Christian church. It is enough, perhaps, to note that the issue is helpfully explored in a recent symposium of the Policy Studies Institute (Modood (ed.), 1997). Parekh, for example, suggests that official acknowledgement of the presence of religious minorities in both the symbols of the state and other expressions of national identity need not preclude a special, privileged relationship between Christianity and the state, for reasons to do with the importance of historical identity and the continuity of cultural ethos (Modood (ed.), 1997, pp. 19f). Other contributors to that volume see a role for the established Church of England in representing and upholding in a public, 'official' way the claims of the sacred, the transcendent, on behalf of the community of Christian churches and the religious minorities.

ECUMENICAL PERSPECTIVES

The issue of establishment arises also in the context of ecumenical dialogue. The Church of England has expressed its readiness to share the opportunities of establishment (such as representation in the

Second Chamber) with other churches and affirms the legitimate place of non-Christian religions in national life and institutions. Its belief in its national mission is undiminished, but it is committed to working with other Chrisian churches in that mission. Establishment need not be exclusive (it is, as I have argued, really a matter of degree). Its basis could be broadened ecumenically. Even other faiths could find a place within the state recognition of religion. We may briefly refer to the question of establishment in relation to the Church of England's closest ecumenical partners, the Roman Catholic, the Methodist and the United Reformed Churches.

THE ROMAN CATHOLIC CHURCH

Though Roman Catholic canon law prohibits clergy from participating in politics and participating in the legislature, the Second Vatican Council did not condemn the principle of state recognition of a church or of establishment as such. How could it when the Roman Catholic Church is effectively established by law, by virtue of concordats with the Holy See, in a number of countries? The Council's *Declaration on Religious Freedom* merely states:

> *If, in view of peculiar circumstances obtaining among certain peoples, special legal recognition is given in the constitutional order of society to one religious body, it is at the same time imperative that the right of all citizens and religious bodies to religious freedom should be recognised and made effective in practice.*
>
> (Abbott (ed.), 1966, p. 685: Dignitatis Humanae: 6)

The Declaration regarded establishment as a contingent matter, dependent on historical circumstances. It neither promoted it nor condemned it.

There is a unique factor in the relations between the Roman Catholic Church and the state. Vatican City is a nation-state in its own right and, by virtue of this fact, it could be said that the Roman Catholic Church at that point is a state church in the fullest possible sense of the word. The loss of the Papal States in the nineteenth century was recouped in principle by the creation of the Vatican City State in 1929. This status enables the Roman Catholic Church in the form of the Holy See to enter into treaties, that are binding in international law, with other sovereign states on an equal basis (Watkin, 1998, p. 91).

Centralizing ('Ultramontane') tendencies during the past century and a half have made it much less likely that the Roman Catholic Church in any particular country would now wish to get involved in the sort of mutual church–state obligations that are entailed in traditional forms of establishment. But that does not mean that the Roman Catholic Church favours the separation of church and state. The classic separation theories of nineteenth-century liberals and socialists were blatant attempts to strip the church of all influence in public life, attempts that the church could not countenance. On the other hand, forms of recognition and partnership that are premised on a constitutional separation of powers, though acceptable, are inferior to the sort of special relationship provided by concordats. Concordats, voluntarily entered into, are by no means a thing of the past. Though the emphasis is on preserving the independence of the church, the principle of reciprocal rights and obligations is the same as in 'establishment' (cf. the useful discussion by Miktat, 1975).

NONCONFORMIST POSITIONS

Nineteenth- and twentieth-century Free Church opposition to establishment drew on earlier separatist and dissenting traditions which had evolved under persecution which was as much political (grounded in concern for the security and cohesion of the realm) as religious (based on a belief in exclusive possession of the truth and its necessity for salvation). Opposition was perpetuated into a different age in a context of continuing civil disadvantage and in an atmosphere of liberal individualism (Sell, 1985). Moderate voices warned of the unintended consequences if disestablishment were to be carried by Free Church agitation. While condemning state control of the church, P. T. Forsyth counselled in 1915: 'Any separation of Church and State which ended in absolute neutrality and mutual indifference would ... mean state paganism – that for the State the Church as a Church had ceased to exist' (cf. Sell, 1985, p. 25). And Daniel Jenkins pointed out, immediately after World War II when a state-sponsored programme of socialism was under way:

> *In a consciously planned society it is by no means certain that a disestablished Church is necessarily the most free. By depressing it to*

the level of a voluntary association among others the State could, if it felt so disposed, effectively neutralize much of its influence.

(cf. Sell, 1985, p. 25)

The report of the Free Church Federal Council's commission on church and state, published in 1953, *The Free Churches and the State* gave qualified support to the principle of establishment in a broad sense and certainly did not find it a stumbling block:

> *Though Free Churchmen reject the State control of religion, they welcome State recognition of religion. We do not desire to see a secular State in England. We hold it right, for example, that public education should be on a Christian basis, and that there should be chaplains in our hospitals and in the armed forces. It is right that on great national occasions, such as a Coronation, there should be solemn acknowledgement by the State of the ultimate Sovereignty of God.*

(Nicholls (ed.), 1967, p. 215)

The report went on to stake a claim, as it were, in establishment: 'It would be easy by ill-considered proposals for disestablishment to jeopardise the existing valuable cooperation between Church and State in which the Free Churches have come increasingly to share' (Nicholls (ed.), 1967, p. 215).

The Methodist Church has frequently affirmed the God-given role of the state, as a fellow-servant with the Church of God and the Kingdom of God, though it has naturally also safeguarded the ultimate spiritual independence of the Church. Methodist statements on church and state have affirmed that the church can uphold and support the state in maintaining justice and liberty, but that it has the clear duty under God to withstand the state if its actions imperil those civic virtues. The record of Methodist partnership with the state, expressed in both word and deed, is impressive. The Methodist Conference has never regarded establishment as unacceptable in principle. The classical nineteenth-century Wesleyans tended to accept it as proper and appropriate for the Church of England, though some of the non-Wesleyan Methodists, who were closer to the Independents in ecclesiology, were strongly opposed both to establishment in principle and to the established Church of England in particular. Now, however, the 'independent' strand within Methodism has been subsumed within the strong connexional ecclesiology which, in principle, might be thought to lend itself to the idea of a national church.

The Anglican–Methodist unity scheme of 1968, approved by the Methodist Conference, envisaged a renewal through unity, without prejudice to its established status, though with some possible modifications that would make it not less self-governing than the Methodist Church itself, for the reunited church. Since then, of course, there have been significant developments in the Church of England's relation to the state, amounting to effective self-government – albeit devolved by Parliament – within the parameters of partnership with the state: fully fledged synodical government in 1970, the power to legislate for doctrine and worship by canon in 1974, and the Crown Appointments Commission that nominates diocesan bishops, as a result of the Chadwick report of 1970. A review of the working – not of the principles – of the vacancy in see arrangements and of the Crown Appointments Commission, in the interests of greater openness and accountability, began work in 1999.

Defining an established church as 'a national Church, constitutionally recognised by the State as the Church of the nation,' the Anglican–Methodist unity scheme pointed out that 'establishment is a relation whereby the State officially acknowledges God in upholding his Church'. The Commission noted that no biblical principle forbids establishment, that the Methodist Church enjoyed the same 'invisible endowments' as the Church of England (exemption from rates and other concessions) and that the Methodist Church manifested 'a national character and spirit to a marked degree' (Anglican–Methodist Unity Commission, 1968, pp. 93, 95). Reunion would be the beginning of the healing of the national church and the relaunching of its mission. The renewed courtship between Anglicans and Methodists that began in the mid-1990s could benefit enormously from picking up the threads of this earlier agreement as far as church and state matters are concerned.

The United Reformed Church, on the other hand, in its 'Basis of Union', seems at first sight hostile to establishment:

> The United Reformed Church declares that the Lord Jesus Christ, the only ruler and head of the Church, has therein appointed a government distinct from civil government and in things spiritual not subordinate thereto, and that civil authorities, being always subject to

*the rule of God, ought to respect the rights of conscience and of
religious belief ...*

(Schedule D, Version 1)

This statement obviously reflects a differentiated society, in which
church and state are separate, distinct bodies, rather than the
integrated commonwealth presupposed by the historic Anglican
formularies and Richard Hooker, in which church and state (spiritual
and temporal) were two aspects of one unified realm, with the
monarch bearing sovereignty in both. But we note the implied
distinction between spiritual and temporal matters and the overriding
concern for freedom of conscience. The thinking here is not far
removed from the thinking that underlies the development of
synodical government in the Church of England.

The United Reformed Church uses a second version of this
declaration in which (while no difference in meaning is intended)
the language of separation between church and state is toned down a
little:

*We believe that Christ gives his Church a government distinct from
the government of the state. In things that affect obedience to God the
Church is not subordinate to the state, but must serve the Lord Jesus
Christ, its only Ruler and Head ...*

The expression 'things that affect obedience to God' seems rather
more specific than 'things spiritual' and perhaps suggests recognition
of an area of 'things indifferent' *(adiaphora)*, a concept favoured by
the Lutheran and Anglican Reformers. It should go without saying
that even Anglicans can only accept a particular working relationship
with the state 'as far as the law of Christ allows'.

If conscience is safeguarded and the relationship to the state that is
involved in establishment does not require disobedience to God, then
perhaps both the Methodist Church and the United Reformed
Church could contemplate further steps to unity with the Church
of England that are not bought at the cost of her disestablishment but
rather would enable each church to share in the pastoral and
prophetic opportunities that establishment brings.

A 'STICKING POINT'?

The one 'sticking point' that offends some Anglicans and some
Nonconformists is the role played by the Crown (in effect by the

Prime Minister) in the appointment of diocesan bishops. By a convention stated in the House of Commons by Prime Minister James Callaghan in 1976, the Prime Minister may choose either of two names submitted by the Crown Appointments Commission or may ask for two more names. The Prime Minister recommends a name to Her Majesty which she is constitutionally bound to accept. The ambiguously named Crown Appointments Commission is in fact a commission of the Church of England's General Synod, comparable to the Liturgical or Doctrine Commissions, not a commission of the Crown. The names have emerged by consultation, on the part of both the church and the Prime Minister's office, within the church and the wider community. It is as though the Prime Minister umpires the process to ensure that certain salutary criteria, accepted by the church but including the interests of the wider community, are met. Within those limits, he or she has a real area of discretion.

I find nothing objectionable in this procedure. The Queen is advised by the Prime Minister in the latter's capacity as the sovereign's First Minister, not as the leader of a political party. That is why the Prime Minister does not need to consult the Cabinet and is not answerable to Parliament for the advice he gives the sovereign on ecclesiastical appointments. The Prime Minister also ex officio bears the responsibility for ensuring that the wider interests of society and the nation are taken into account. This seems entirely appropriate for a national, established church. A church that could not come up with two names, either of which would be acceptable to the church and the vacant diocese, would be in a pretty parlous state as far as its leadership is concerned. No doubt there could be improvements in the detailed mechanics of this process, particularly in the direction of a greater openness that was not bought at the expense of confidentiality, but personally I cannot see that any issue of principle is at stake. The Prime Minister can only recommend to the sovereign the name of a candidate whom the church itself has proposed and whom the Archbishop is willing to consecrate. To all intents and purposes the church chooses its own chief pastors.

8

Towards a United National Church in Mission

We have already taken to heart the ambiguity of the expression 'national church'. We have made it clear that we are not promoting the idea of a nationalistic, chauvinistic or ethnically exclusive church. What remains vital in this idea, when all qualifications and caveats have been acknowledged, is the imperative of mission and ministry within a nation and a society in every part and at every level. This aspiration, I want to stress, is not confined to established, territorial churches, though it is likely to be stronger and more enduring in their case because it is undergirded by history, law and custom. In our present circumstances, heading towards a post-Christian society, churches that share this aspiration should work together to fulfil it. Given our current sense of how mission and unity belong together, it is theologically inappropriate as well as anachronistic for any one church to attempt this alone. Not only do neither the Church of England nor the Church of Scotland have a monopoly of Christian allegiance. If we take into account both Roman Catholics and Free Church people, together with those of other faiths, they do not any more enjoy the majority allegiance of active Christian practice in their respective nations.

Clearly the Church of England is not the national church today in the sense that it is the church of all the people of the nation. Since the Reformation it has never been that. It may be the largest church numerically, having baptized about half of the population, but that proportion is reducing. There are probably as many Roman Catholics at mass as there are Anglicans worshipping in their parish churches

and cathedrals. Neither is the Church of England the national or
state church in the sense that the nation, through its elected political
institutions, controls or governs the church. The Church of England
has virtually full autonomy in doctrine, worship and discipline. Yet
she still aspires to serve the nation as a whole and does not really see
herself as one denomination among others. So in what sense, other
than by virtue of legal establishment, may the Church of England be
regarded as a national church?

The total pastoral constituency of the Church of England includes
the spiritual and communal life represented by about 20,000 parish
churches and chapels and 43 cathedrals (the forty-fourth, though
certainly within the Church of England, being in Gibraltar), a quarter
of all primary schools, a number of church colleges of higher
education, chaplaincies in innumerable institutions, schools and
colleges of Anglican foundation and the work of Anglican societies
in the voluntary sector. Within those parishes and sector ministries
we should take account of the large numbers of individuals, couples,
families and groups who are in receipt of pastoral care, support and
guidance. Pastoral contact is maintained through parochial visiting,
the occasional offices, Sunday Schools, church youth groups, the
Mothers' Union, uniformed organizations and open church buildings.
Through festivals and the convivial activity that celebrates them (e.g.
harvest suppers) many who are not regular churchgoers participate in
the liturgical life of the church. This vast pastoral constituency is
ministered to by nearly 10,000 stipendiary clergy, thousands of non-
stipendiary and active retired clergy, 10,000 Readers and thousands
of recognized lay assistants – not to mention something over a
hundred bishops. I suggest that there is a real and serious sense in
which the Church of England is still the national church. But that is
certainly no cause for complacency or arrogance. We should be
acutely aware of how much is not being done, how many individuals
and families are not in touch with the church, and of the
ineffectiveness of our Christian contribution to public doctrine and
national mores.

What the report of the Archbishops' Commission on church and
state ('the Chadwick Report') said in 1970 is still true today: 'The
Church of England is committed, by its history, its name, and its
heritage, to a national mission. No amendment of the laws could alter
the vocation to a national mission' ([Chadwick], 1970, p. 11,
para. 32).

Much, however, has changed in the 30 years since the last commission on church and state did its work. The late Anthony Dyson criticized the four church and state reports that have appeared during the past century (Selborne 1917, Cecil 1935, Moberly 1952, Chadwick 1970) for a lack of theological principle. He points to their dominant historical-legal-consitutional approach, condemning it as a 'confused, unprincipled nexus', lacking in prophetic critique: the 'formation of theological principle by historical anomaly'. I trust that our discussion of church and state questions, premised as it is on the theological connection between unity and mission, will not incur the same criticism. Significantly for our purposes, Dyson detected a lack of ecumenical seriousness, of a readiness to allow the fruits of the ecumenical movement, which were already quite apparent by 1970 when the unity discussions between the Church of England and the Methodist Church were at a crucial stage, to shape the conception of a national church (Dyson in Moyser (ed.), 1985, pp. 299-309). My argument here moves towards the vision of a truly united national church.

The urgent background to our discussion is the brute fact of decline. 'The most important single characteristic of the Church of England in the twentieth century has been the catastrophic numerical decline in its active membership' (Hinton, 1994, p. 12). Particularly since 1970 the Church of England as an institution has continued to decline by every variable that one might care to measure, though there has been a recovery in one or two areas (notably numbers being ordained and recommended for ordination training) recently. The Church of England managed to lose half its effective constituency in the 25 years between 1960 and 1985. Whenever the future of the national church, or its possible disestablishment, has been discussed – whether in the 1830s or 1930s – the numerical strength of the Church of England has been weighed in the balance. There is no getting away from numbers. Hensley Henson (at the time still a doughty supporter of establishment) warned in a sermon in Westminster Abbey in 1907 that 'a national church which is not the organ of a national Christianity is an unreality, perhaps even a fraud: and that disastrous state may be reached by the fault of the church not less surely than by the fault of the nation' (Henson, 1908, p. 17). Until now, the Church of England has been able to claim the nominal affiliation of the majority of the population. That may not be true much longer. With the reduction in the numbers of infant baptisms, the great rump of nominal

Anglicans will inevitably diminish. It is appalling that church electoral rolls represent a tiny fraction of the population. It seems an urgent priority to increase the quantity as well as the quality of Anglican allegiance. This can only be done by extending the church's involvement in the diverse patterns of community that are now characteristic of our postmodern, fragmented, but not community-less society.

Numerical decline is related to other changes in the church and society. The rise of evangelicalism, especially charismatic evangelicalism, though it has strengthened the impact of the Church of England in mission, has sometimes brought with it a careless attitude to church structures beyond the congregation, combined with lack of interest in ecclesiology. It has often tended to create a firmer boundary between the church and the community through more rigorous baptism policy, for example. At the same time, society is more secular and the churches are more marginal. The Roman Catholic Church has consolidated its place in national life. Sectarian violence in Northern Ireland has had a seriously discrediting effect on the churches. Other faiths, such as Islam, are stronger and more articulate than they were. Alternative spiritualities dominate the market for faith. What can it mean to be a national, established church in a deeply pluralist society? The answer I want to offer can be put in five points.

WHAT MIGHT A NATIONAL, ESTABLISHED AND UNITED CHURCH MEAN TODAY?

A defence against secularism

A national, established church is a defence against the complete secularization of the constitution. The link between church and nation, embodied in the special place of the Church of England, means that the constitution is not avowedly secular (as it is in France and the United States, for example). It implies a national recognition of the Christian religion and a religious basis for national life. The provisions of the 1944 and 1988 Education Acts, which between them required religious education and a daily act of collective worship of a mainly Christian character, indicate that such national recognition is still forthcoming and is thought to be important.

Behind such legislation lies the theological insight that the state is, as Scripture and the theological tradition of the Church clearly teach, a God-given institution which, as such, can mediate, imperfectly, the divine order. It is still possible to conceive of a Christian society and a Christian basis for the state, that is to say, one that gives the state moral and spiritual responsibilities that are imbued with values derived from the Judeo-Christian tradition, without threatening the freedom under the law of other religious bodies, but rather serving to guarantee them.

Keith Ward has developed this line of reasoning in a particularly helpful way (Ward, 1992). A state may not wish to be completely secular. It may wish to acknowledge spiritual values. A wise people will know that this cannot be done in the abstract, by affirming spirituality in general or faith as such, or all faiths, whatever they may be. It will realize that this can only be done concretely and specifically, by recognizing a particular religious tradition or church. Not all religions or churches will be suitable for this purpose. A suitable religion for state recognition will be tolerant and hospitable to insights from beyond itself. It will provide ceremonial enactments of its beliefs that are symbolically satisfying and morally effective. It will hold its central truths with conviction, but allow for diversity of interpretation. Finally, it will sustain values that are widely shared and can support consensus and help to build up communities. So Ward concludes:

> It is a good thing to have a religion established by law as long as most members of a state take religious questions seriously, as long as dissent is permitted, as long as the established religion is concerned to encourage constructive conversations with other religious communities, to permit diversity of interpretation within itself and to show a concern to formulate a broad value base for the state as a whole.
>
> (Ward, 1992, p. 16)

This portrait sounds very much like Anglican aspirations at their best! The established status of the Church of England remains a constitutional defence against the complete secularization of the state. In a moment we shall ask how the Free Churches could be more closely involved in this.

A voice in national policy

The existence of a national, established church means that the Christian perspective has a recognized place in the sphere of public doctrine. In a pluralist society the Church cannot insist that all citizens should profess Christian beliefs and follow a Christian way of life. But it can still expect Christian truth to be reflected in the law of the land. Certainly, as the established church, its voice has a right to be heard as a contribution to debate, as a shaping factor and as way of ensuring, to say the very least, that legislation is not framed that is a flagrant denial of Christian moral principles. The formal recognition of a church and its theological tradition (including its moral theology) creates a framework within which the Christian contribution has a secure place.

John Habgood has called this framework 'public faith' and defined it as composed of 'the things which bind us together, and the values we share, and the goals we pursue'. Public faith is, according to Habgood, 'the framework of assumptions, mostly drawn from the great historic expressions of religious faith, which makes the public articulation of personal faith both possible and fruitful' (Habgood, 1988, pp. 8, 11). Public discourse is helped to make these assumptions congenial to the Christian faith, because the biblical and theological tradition is concretely enshrined in the recognized role of the national, established church. Such salutary assumptions do not float about in the ether, but are embodied in institutions and the moral communities that sustain them (MacIntyre, 1985; Gill, 1992). Duncan Forrester has highlighted, from within the established Church of Scotland, the need for a political theology for a post-Christendom situation. But he has insisted at the same time that 'a political theology must stay resolutely in the public realm and must engage with the ideologies, structures and practices that are to be found there' (Forrester, 1988). That admirable sentiment suggests the question: how can this be achieved except by the Church being engaged precisely ideologically, structurally and practically – in other words, being radically incarnated in the public realm and public discourse?

Within the framework that provides the parameters of discourse, the church will sometimes be called to engage in prophetic critique, either of trends in society or (in exceptional circumstances) of government policies (I have mentioned the serious constraints on the latter in Hannaford (ed.), 1998). Now anyone can set themselves up as a prophet and people can choose whether or not to listen to them. But a society that gives a recognized role to a specific Christian theological tradition cannot plausibly ignore the prophetic voice when it is raised in its midst, though it may find the message unpalatable. The prophets of ancient Israel emerged from within the national church, so to speak, and addressed the nation that was at the same time the church. The fact that a national church is identified (though not uncritically) with the national community, affirms it as far as it can, and works with the grain of the tradition of that moral community as far as possible, puts it in a strong position when it feels bound to strike a discordant note. A 'loyal opposition' carries considerable moral weight, all the more for the encompassing sense of identification, solidarity and commitment (on prophetic intervention, see Gill, 1981).

Rowan Williams (Archbishop of a national but disestablished, though partly endowed, church: the Church in Wales) has described the essential task of theological interpretation, on the basis of Scripture, as engaging in public interaction leading to the articulation of judgements that are intended to affect public discourse and consequently social life. The intervention of Christian prophetic speech will be orientated towards moments of shared discourse and common purpose in society, but without endorsing them uncritically (Williams, 1989, pp. 92ff, 98, 103). A non-established church with a national profile, such as the Church in Wales or the Roman Catholic Church in England and Wales, of course has a recognized voice. A national and established church, such as the Church of England or the (Presbyterian) Church of Scotland, has not only a recognized voice but a platform from which to speak and a right to be heard, if not always heeded. (For a comparison of Scottish and English experiences of being a national church, see Bradley, 'The Role of a National Church: a view from across the Border', in Warren (ed.), 1992; cf. also Forrester, 1999.)

Keith Clements' *Learning to Speak: The Church's Voice in Public Affairs* (Clements, 1995) has wise advice on this point. The Church should be reticent about 'speaking out', Clements believes. It should eschew the fantasy that it can offer a solution to every problem. It needs to listen and learn before uttering. Its most constructive role is to engage in dialogue and to ask questions that evoke a transcendent, spiritual context for political decisions. The Church should not ask 'What can we say?' without at the same time asking 'What can we do?' Altogether Clements advocates a fairly minimal prophetic witness for the Church in society. Though the realism and humility of his approach is well taken, I have a suspicion that he underestimates the importance of church leaders stating the obvious. In an increasingly secular society, truths that are almost platitudes to committed Christians need to be stated and repeated and people well beyond the worshipping life of the Church long to hear them.

Prophecy is not a matter of uttering isolated oracles: discrete messages of judgement could not be heard unless against a backcloth of Christian meaning. Prophecy is an holistic not a sporadic activity of the Church, an intrinsic, not a contingent ministry. Just as the whole life of the Church is priestly and kingly or royal, so it is also prophetic. As O'Donovan says: 'Out of all its vocations the church prophesies: its administration, its charity, its music, its art, its theology, its politics, its religious ecstasy, its preaching.' Though there are individual prophetic voices, they do not address the world directly, but first they speak to the Church. 'There is no *private* Christian counsel to be delivered to the principalities and powers, bypassing their need to confront the social reality of the Church' (O'Donovan, 1996, p. 188).

A national mission

To be a national, established church means that the church serves the nation as a whole and every constituent community of it. It has a ministry of word, sacrament and pastoral care that is extended nationwide. It maintains its places of worship in every significant community. It does not – and knows it cannot – retreat from the inner city or remote rural areas, where support is weak compared to the suburbs and market towns, but regards these as missionary opportunities. It is morally and legally obligated to continue to provide its pastoral ministry there, in the form of sacred persons, sacred places and sacred events.

A national, established church has a mission and a ministry not only to the nation as a whole and to every constituent community through the parochial structure (with citizens having a corresponding claim on the pastoral services of the church), but also to people of all degrees of spiritual maturity or immaturity. It recognizes pilgrims at various stages of their journey, including those who have just set out and those who have wandered from the beaten path, as its proper concern. A national, established church, which is by definition a community church, is capacious enough to accommodate all shades of commitment. It embraces within its care those on the far reaches of the penumbra who come to church only occasionally and make contact mainly through the rites of passage as well as those who form the dedicated inner core of personnel who keep parish activities going. It leads the former back to their Christian heritage and nurtures the latter from the springs of traditional spirituality. As David Martin has written, a national church

> *holds a door open for whoever wants to enter holy space or to overhear its messages from the outer court . . . a national Church is a presence conveying memory and continuity. In it you find a special kind of commemorative re-presentation, not casual amnesia.*

> (Martin, 1997, p. 245)

The defence of establishment in the face of the threat from the radical Utilitarians in the 1830s was based on the record of the Church of England's service to the nation, specially in education and pastoral ministrations to all who were willing to receive them. Bishop Blomfield of London was convinced that, as long as the Church of England retained its national mission, particularly as 'the instructress of the people', its position was secure. At this time, Gladstone too saw establishment primarily as a pastoral opportunity: to bring the pastoral ministrations of the church to the 'congregated masses of misery and ignorance' (Brose, 1959, pp. 35, 59). Gladstone's words may sound quaint and patronizing, but on reflection they are actually just as pertinent a century and a half later.

If the Church of England should ever renounce its mission to the whole nation, withdraw its clergy from those communities that cannot provide full financial support for them, start to close down parish churches where they are not well supported, and erect barriers to parishioners coming for baptism, marriage and funeral services, it will have abdicated the very role that secures its special position in the nation and facilitates its distinctive mission. By turning its back on large pastoral and evangelistic opportunities, it will have shown that it no longer regards itself as a national church. Disestablishment and disendowment will inevitably follow, either by positive legislation or by gradual erosion. It will have started on the downward path that eventually leads to the sectarian mentality. It will not deserve to survive.

Commitment to community

Every national church is committed to its environing community and an established church particularly so. It cannot be inward-looking or take a semi-detached attitude to national, social and communal affairs. The Anglican tradition presupposes that the grace of God is at work in the world and that God is involved in the creation of all true community. It seeks to bring about, in Dan Hardy's words, 'the embodiment of graced sociality'. It is called to bring the grace of God into a definitive focus by mediating it, not just in the private lives of its individual members, but through its very institutions, though without absolutizing them.

On principle, the Anglican understanding of the Church is not held without reference to civil society. When Anglicans talk about the church they do not talk about the church alone. There are four ways in which Anglicans speak of the church: the parish, the diocese, the national church and the catholic Church, the Church of Christ. Each of these implies a valuation of the broader communities that it entails. The parish places a value on the local community. The diocese entails a valuation of the county, city or region. A national church implies a valuation of the nation, its history, culture and identity. And the idea of the catholic Church sets a value on the unity of the human race and incorporates a vision of global community.

This moral valuation, brought by the Church to every level of community to which it is committed, comprises a regard for history, tradition, creativity, territory and networks of affiliation, kinship and common concerns. It privileges the constellation of values that give an abiding identity to a community. This is precisely the sphere in which the mission of Anglican churches operates. It means that a parish, a diocese or a national church does not see the sphere of its mission as a purely geographical one, that can be measured and divided up into manageable portions, but as a moral, spiritual, personal, communal and cultural one.

Through the centuries Anglicans have maintained that God has a purpose for nations and cultures and that one of the functions of the Church is to help to evoke that purpose. Peter Sedgwick has recently affirmed that the strength of Anglican polity is its determination to affect the whole of life, in each particular town, village or suburb, paying attention to the precise particularity of each location. He therefore believes that 'Anglican polity can seek to retain a central place in national life, despite the secularity of our society, if it is committed to a full engagement with the social change which constantly surrounds it' (Sedgwick, pp. 199, 208; cf. Hardy in the same volume, p. 339; where he states that the 'embodiment of graced sociality' is the 'fundamental rationale for Anglican polity').

At a time when sectarian tendencies within the Church of England, in the form of restricted baptism or even marriage policy, congregationalist attitudes vis-à-vis the diocese and its bishop, are beginning to rear their ugly head, it is all the more imperative to insist that Anglicanism is inherently and eradicably non-sectarian and should never become preoccupied with its own purity and oblivious to the Christ who goes about among sinners, the poor, the sick and the disturbed. Anglicanism's *raison d'être* is given by reference to the environing human community wherever it is placed.

It is important to see that this intended orientation of Anglican ecclesiology to the community it serves is not necessarily dependent on legal establishment, though it is bound up with the ideal of a national church and an intensive territorial ministry that may not be possible without historic endowments. The Church of England may be the only church of the Anglican Communion that is fully established, but it is not the only instantiation of this distinctive Anglican polity (a polity that is distinctive of Anglicanism though not exclusive to it) because, as I have already mentioned, Anglican churches have consistently wished to see themselves as national churches. Bruce Kaye, of the Anglican Church of Australia, in his recent book *A Church Without Walls*, has affirmed that Anglicanism, wherever it is found, is authentically a 'Church in society' type of Christianity in which the knowledge of God is personal but not private and which is deeply implicated in the structures and problems of society on the analogy of the incarnation (Kaye, 1996, pp. 103, 146f).

A truly national, united church

Given the intimate theological connection between mission and unity (cf. chapter 1), a national, established church must be a truly united church, one that proclaims with undivided voice 'one Lord, one faith, one baptism, one God and Father of all' (Ephesians 4.5-6) and is effectively the catalyst for progressively fuller forms of Christian unity. We need now to ask, 'What is the relevance of the ecumenical movement – that movement of greater understanding and abounding goodwill that now exists between still separated churches – to the future of a national church?'

Some historians have suggested that the ideal of a truly national church came closest to being realized in the reign of James I, that is to say, in the first quarter of the seventeenth century, and was almost immediately lost again, when the aggressive policies of Charles I and Archbishop Laud undermined the cohesion of nation and church. In this period Anglican divines tended to distinguish between Presbyterians, who were regarded as the acceptable face of dissent, and who might be comprehended within the national church, and 'other sectaries' (Independents, Baptists, Quakers), who could not. The touchstone was ecclesiology: whether the ecclesiological centre of gravity lay in the gathered local congregation or was distributed more widely (more connexionally we might say, borrowing a key Methodist term), in the diocese and national church.

But many bishops were not willing to make the compromises necessary for a truly comprehensive church (N. Sykes, 1959, ch. 3: 'Comprehension Versus Toleration'). By the rigours of the Act of Uniformity 1662, 2,000 ministers (mostly Presbyterians but some Independents) were ejected from the livings they had acquired (in most cases entirely legitimately) during the Commonwealth.

There was an opportunity to repair this breach, at least as far as moderate Nonconformists were concerned, at the Revolution in 1688–89. But by settling for toleration of dissent within the law, instead of comprehension of differences in a united church, the Church of England conceded freedom of worship while holding on to political power. As Spurr comments, the Church of England became no longer a national church, in the full sense of the word, but merely an established church; it retained the power and privilege without the underlying rationale (cf. Spurr, 1991, pp. 103ff). I want to ask (as Thomas Arnold, S. T. Coleridge and F. D. Maurice did in the early nineteenth century) whether what is still a national established church can once again become truly the church of the English people. This is my Anglican question with an ecumenical answer, for I do not believe that it can happen without the other churches and without healing the wounds of the past.

In his evidence to the 1935 commission on church and state, Norman Sykes astutely pointed out that, since establishment in a pluralist society is of grace, not of right, its continuance depends on the goodwill of the Free Churches – in fact, on what he calls 'a concordat' or *entente cordiale* with Nonconformity. Should the

Protestant churches or, more realistically today, the Roman Catholic Church, ever wish to make an issue of establishment, it would immediately become vulnerable. Norman Sykes concluded that the Church of England could not rise to the full realization of its aspiration as the *Ecclesia Anglorum*, the Church of the English, without reunion with the Protestant Nonconformist churches ([Cecil], 1936, pp. 297–300). In the same spirit, I take the future of a national church with a truly national mission to be one of the most urgent contexts for the current discussions between the Church of England and the Protestant churches severally. We can pursue this issue by addressing several questions.

First we need to ask whether the sense in which the Church of England today sees itself as a national church is shared by the other major churches in England. This question can be answered broadly in the affirmative. If Anglicans aspire to be a church for the community, so do most Nonconformist churches. If Anglicans are not a gathered church but offer their ministrations to all who will receive them, so too do most Nonconformists. If Anglicans seek to have a role and a voice in the life of the nation, so too do the Nonconformist churches and the Roman Catholics. There are parts of England where the church that is central for the community and is taken for granted in a quasi-established way is not an Anglican one. If Anglicans and other churches – the Nonconformist churches particularly – share this sense of vocation they should act to carry it out together. Surely a greater partnership in pastoral ministry is possible? The Church of England's distinctive relationship to the state need not exclude other churches that are willing to be associated with her in this task.

In Scotland, ecumenical developments through the Scottish Initiative for Unity (SCIFU), if they succeed, will surely bring the non-established Anglican and Nonconformist churches into union with the established Church of Scotland in such a way that they will come to share its national mission through a territorial ministry and therefore its established status. I assume that this is clear to the non-presbyterian churches and that the Church of Scotland welcomes this possibility.

There are, however, differences that need to be smoothed out. They concern the pastoral implications of being, as the Church of England is and the non-Anglican churches in England are not, at least in the same way, a territorial church with a pastoral obligation, not merely to any who may approach it for its ministrations, but to all who are willing to receive them as offered at large in the community. (The same issue applies *mutatis mutandis* in Scotland.) To many Anglicans the parish means not a line on a map but a specific quantum of pastoral responsibility. Many Anglican clergy and lay church representatives call routinely and systematically on newcomers to the parish. They visit the sick, whether or not they attend church. The clergy perform baptisms and marriages for those parishioners who ask for these ministrations in sincerity and conduct funeral services for deceased parishioners even if they were not church people. This is not Anglican imperialism or an assumption of 'effortless superiority': it is the *raison d'être* of a pastoral ministry to the whole community. It is not exclusive to the Church of England, but it is the emphasis, the centre of gravity, that is distinctive.

Those who are uneasy with this time-honoured aspect of Anglican ministry might ask themselves whether they believe in a universal pastoral mission or not. Is this approach compatible with the ministry of Nonconformist church ministers which in practice tends to be primarily (but by no means exclusively) to their own scattered membership? These differences are not absolute, but are a matter of degree. They are not an insuperable barrier if, as they justly claim, the Free Churches do indeed see their mission as being to the whole surrounding community. A significantly greater degree of visible unity would provide an opportunity to deliver that mission more fully and effectively. Further steps towards visible unity, grounded in theological convergence, could result in a broadening of the national church, bringing greater pastoral opportunities to the ministers and active lay people of the Free Churches and a greater recognition of their role and voice in the nation, in conjunction with that of the Church of England.

The argument of this chapter is intended to support the contention that there is now little or nothing in the established status of the Church of England to which the Nonconformist churches or the Roman Catholic Church (let alone Anglicans themselves) could reasonably object on principle. 'Establishment' is just a word, and a highly ambiguous one at that. The reality to which it points does not seem to me to be controversial. Virtually all Christian traditions aspire to be involved with the institutions that comprise civil society. They welcome co-operation with the state, which they acknowledge on the basis of Scripture to be a divinely ordained institution. They are thankful when the state offers some kind of formal recognition of their contribution to the nation.

The working relationship between the state and the churches is a matter of degree and its exact form is shaped by historical contingencies. All churches are constrained to function within the framework of the law and in theory their judicial processes can be enforced by the courts. The state can intervene in the 'internal' affairs of any church if the public interest demands it. Establishment – if we must use that loaded word – is not a clear-cut notion. Churches that relate to the state, in some or all of its present diverse expressions, are more or less 'established', by virtue of the degree to which they enjoy state recognition and the degree to which they accept an obligation entrusted to them by the state, to sustain a national mission in the form of a ministry of word, sacrament and pastoral care.

Recent developments in the ideas of nationhood and of statehood actually call for a closer relationship between the church and these bodies. Let us not imagine that nationhood is outmoded or that the day of the nation-state is over. It is still true that 'only religious attachments have rivalled national loyalties in their scope and fervour' (Hutchinson and Smith (eds), 1994, p. 4) and when religious commitment and national emotion are combined the result is explosive. New nation-states are continually coming to birth as politico-economic power blocs disintegrate, as in Yugoslavia and the Soviet Union (cf. David Owen in Platten (ed.), 1999). The resurgence of national aspirations, whether in the strong form in Eastern Europe or the weak form in Britain and Ireland, is a response to the global levelling and homogenizing of cultures, the collapse of totalitarian economies, and the curtailing of sovereignty in trans-national economic or political groupings.

Identity is the crux of these developments. As Renan argued in a classic statement on nationhood, a nation is above all a moral community with a distinct historical consciousness. The desire of a nation to be together is the touchstone of nationhood for Renan (Hutchinson and Smith (eds), 1994, pp. 15ff). Resurgent national consciousness is related to the springs of collective identity which are deeply rooted in tradition. For many nations, not least those of Eastern Europe but also those of the United Kingdom, that tradition is ineradicably shaped by the Christian Church and its theological tradition. It is interesting to note that levels of belonging to a religion and of the importance of God in one's life (though not of actual churchgoing) in Eastern and Western Europe are on a par (Gallup International Millennium Survey, 1999).

Acute questions are raised for the English nation (part of the British state) by recent developments. The concomitant processes of simultaneous fragmentation and centralization that have been taking place in Europe as a whole are now being replicated in the United Kingdom. While Scotland and Wales have national fora with specific powers (Northern Ireland's is in the balance at the time of writing this), which can serve as the voice of national identity and aspirations, there is nothing in the proposed regional devolution of government in England that equates to these. Max Weber insisted that nationhood entailed being committed to a particular political project (Hutchinson and Smith (eds), 1994, p. 15). What such project is available to England? As such questions begin to sink in, they will surely generate considerable heart-searching about the identity, purpose and common interests of England and the English. Recent writings show that this is already happening among a section of the intelligentsia (e.g. Marr, 2000). What will the Church of England, which from the sixteenth century has played a crucial role in the continuing formation of English nationhood which can be seen at work as far back as Alfred and Bede (see Hastings, 1997), be able to contribute to this discussion?

Similarly with the state, considered as the perduring constitutional, legal and organizational structure of the nation: the state is now, paradoxically, both more dispersed and at the same time more ubiquitous, more amorphous and yet more pervasive. Non-governmental public organizations and quangos, partnerships with private finance initiatives and other private enterprise contractors in the delivery of public services, support for and reliance on charities and other agencies in the voluntary sector, the devolving of national, regional and local government within limits strictly specified by the state – all these developments play their part in mediating the power of the state and extending it into more and more areas of communal life, while at the same time diluting its direct authority. Although national sovereignty is increasingly compromised and the socialist ideal of a state-run economy is discredited, the pre-economic function of the state as the regulating, monitoring, supervising and shaping force in society is more extensive than ever, though in dispersed, negotiated and insidious ways (see Hazell (ed.), 1999; Platten (ed.), 1999).

Engagement with the state at various levels has become unavoidable for the Church, as for all historic institutions and voluntary organizations. The churches cannot stand back, even supposing they should want to. Various patterns of partnership, with necessary safeguards of the Church's vital spiritual integrity, are now more appropriate and necessary than for some time past. Faced with such opportunities and demands, the churches should not be coy of involvement with the state, and certainly should not react emotively to the word 'establishment'. The unique relationship that established churches, such as the Church of England and the Church of Scotland, have with the state – nationally, parochially and in civic life – could be a bridgehead for an enhanced national recognition and a reaffirmed national responsibility for other churches, especially the Free Churches, in growing unity with the established church.

There is now little or nothing in the Church of England's relationship to the state to which properly informed Nonconformist Christians could take exception. This established church is fully conciliar in government and has authority in its doctrine, worship and discipline. The long-stop of Parliament on synodical measures, in the interests of the rights and well-being of all citizens, and the limited role of the Prime Minister in the appointment of bishops, can be salutary. They can (in Martyn Percy's telling phrase) prevent the church running away with itself: second thoughts are sometimes better than first thoughts. The churches today are actually very much in the same boat, with regard to church–state relations, whatever they may like to think.

Is it completely misguided, then, to envisage a broadening of the idea of a national church, where establishment is not an issue, in a way that would enable the major Nonconformist churches to become more effective national churches – or rather, to become one truly national church in fellowship, in union with the Church of England? The Anglican–Methodist Unity scheme of 1968 observed that 'until all the Churches have come together in a closer unity, there cannot be a fully national Church'. It went on to suggest that Anglican–Methodist unity would constitute 'a step towards the reintegration of the broken national Church of this land, with a view to its renewal for mission and ministry to the whole of our national community and every area of national life'. The Commission envisaged other churches eventually coming to share in the restored national church and participating in principle in the historic church-state relationship (Anglican–Methodist Unity Commission, 1968, pp. 93, 96, 98).

Today we are perhaps less optimistic about schemes for total union and more inclined to favour a steady step-by-step approach. But even this has significant implications for the mission of a united national church. Closer collaboration in the national mission would go hand in hand with a progressively fuller mutual acknowledgement of each other as true and apostolic churches of Christ. On the basis of the mission imperative, the Church of England, the Nonconformist churches and the Roman Catholic Church (so far as that is possible) should embark on a greater partnership in the national mission, grounded of course in solid theological agreement, and involving the sharing and strengthening of the pastoral and prophetic opportunities provided by the Church of England's unique position in the nation.

Bibliography

Abbott, W. M. (ed.), 1966. *The Documents of Vatican II*, London, Geoffrey Chapman.

Anglican–Methodist International Commission, 1996. *Sharing in the Apostolic Communion*, Lake Junaluska NC, World Methodist Council.

Anglican–Methodist Unity Commission, 1968. *Anglican–Methodist Unity, 2: The Scheme*, London, SPCK and Epworth Press.

Arnold, T., 1845. *Miscellaneous Works*, London.

Arnold, T., 1874. *Introductory Lectures on Modern History with the Inaugural Lecture*, 6th edn, London.

Aston, N. (ed.), 1997. *Religious Change in Europe 1650–1914*, Oxford, Clarendon Press.

Avis, P. D. L., 1981. *The Church in the Theology of the Reformers*, London, Marshall, Morgan & Scott.

Avis, P. D. L., 1989. *Anglicanism and the Christian Church*, Edinburgh, T. & T. Clark; Minneapolis, Fortress Press.

Avis, P. D. L., 2000. *The Anglican Understanding of the Church: An Introduction*, London, SPCK.

Bagehot, W., 1963. *The English Constitution*, Ithaca NY, Cornell University Press [1867].

Barendt, E., 1998. *An Introduction to Constitutional Law*, Oxford, OUP.

Barth, J. R., 1969. *Coleridge on Christian Doctrine*, Cambridge MA, Harvard University Press.

Bennett, G. V., 1988. 'The Royal Supremacy' in *To the Church of England*, Worthing, Churchman.

Bogdanor, V., 1995. *The Monarchy and the Constitution*, Oxford, Clarendon Press.

Bray, G. (ed.), 1998. *The Anglican Canons 1529–1947*, The Boydell Press/Church of England Record Society.

[Bridge], 1997. *Synodical Government in the Church of England: A Review*, London, Church House Publishing.

Brose, O., 1959. *Church and Parliament: The Reshaping of the Church of England 1828–1860*, Stanford CA, Stanford University Press; London, OUP.

Brueggemann, W., 1978. *The Prophetic Imagination*, Philadelphia, Fortress Press.

Buchanan, C. O., 1994. *Cut the Connection: Disestablishment and the Church of England*, London, Darton, Longman & Todd.

Burke, E., 1834. *An Appeal from the New to the Old Whigs* in *The Works of the Right Hon. Edmund Burke*, vol. 1, London, Holdsworth and Ball.

Burke, E., 1910. *Reflections on the Revolution in France*, London, Dent (Everyman).

Burnham, F. B. (ed.), 1989. *Postmodern Theology: Christian Faith in a Pluralistic World*, San Francisco, Harper & Row.

Butler, P., 1982. *Gladstone: Church, State and Tractarianism*, Oxford, Clarendon Press.

Called to Love and Praise, 1999. Peterborough, Methodist Publishing House.

Calvin, J., n.d. *Institutes of the Christian Religion*, tr. H. Beveridge, London, James Clarke, vol. 2.

Cargill Thompson, W. D. J., 1972. 'The Philosopher of the Politic Society: Richard Hooker as a Political Thinker' in W. Speed Hill (ed.), *Studies in Richard Hooker*, Cleveland and London, The Press of Case Western Reserve University.

Carr, W., 1999. 'A Developing Establishment', *Theology* CII, No. 805 (1999), pp. 2-10.

[Cecil], 1936. *Church and State: Report of the Archbishop's Commission on the Relations between Church and State 1935*, London, Church Assembly.

[Chadwick], 1970. *Church and State: Report of the Archbishops' Commission*, London, CIO.

Chadwick, O., 1983. *Hensley Henson*, Oxford, Oxford University Press.

Chadwick, O., 1987. *The Victorian Church*, London, SCM Press.

Church of Scotland, 1999. 'Submission from the Church of Scotland to the Royal Commission on Reform of the House of Lords', Edinburgh.

Clark, J. C. D., 1985. *English Society 1688-1832*, Cambridge, Cambridge University Press.

Clements, K., 1995. *Learning to Speak: The Church's Voice in Public Affairs*, Edinburgh, T. & T. Clark.

Cobban, A., 1960. *Edmund Burke and the Revolt against the Eighteenth Century*, 2nd edn, London.

Coleman, R., 1992. *Resolutions of the Twelve Lambeth Conferences 1867–1988*, Toronto, Anglican Book Centre.

Coleridge, S. T., 1884. *Table Talk*, ed. H. Morley, London, Routledge.

Coleridge, S. T., 1912. *Poetical Works*, Oxford, Oxford University Press.

Coleridge, S. T., 1976. *On the Constitution of Church and State*, ed. J. Colmar (Collected Works 10: Bollingen Series LXXV), London, Routledge & Kegan Paul; Princeton, Princeton University Press.

Collinson, P., 1982. *The Religion of Protestants: The Church in English Society 1559–1625*, Oxford, Clarendon Press.

Commitment to Mission and Unity, 1996. London, Church House Publishing; Peterborough, Methodist Publishing House.

Cranmer, T., *Remains*, Parker Society edition of the works of the English Reformers, Cambridge, 1840–.

Creighton, L., 1904. *Life and Letters of Mandell Creighton*, 2 vols, London, Longmans, Green & Co.

Creighton, M., 1901. *The Church and the Nation: Charges and Addresses*, London, Longmans, Green & Co.

Cullmann, O., 1957. *The State in the New Testament*, London, SCM Press.

Doe, N., 1996. *The Legal Framework of the Church of England*, Oxford, Clarendon Press.

Doe, N., 1998. *Canon Law in the Anglican Communion*, Oxford, Clarendon Press.

Dunstan, G. R., 1982. 'Corporate Union and the Body Politic' in M. Santer (ed.), *Their Lord and Ours*, London, SPCK, pp. 129–48.

Eliot, T. S., 1939. *The Idea of a Christian Society*, London, Faber.

Elizabeth I, 1559. *Injunctions Given by the Queen's Majesty As well to the Clergy as to the Laity of this Realm*, London.

Elton, G. R., 1972. *The Tudor Constitution: Documents and Commentary*, Cambridge, Cambridge University Press.

Fallows, W. G., 1964. *Mandell Creighton and the English Church*, London, Oxford University Press.

Figgis, J. N., 1913. *Churches in the Modern State*, London, Longmans, Green & Co.

Figgis, J. N., 1922. *The Divine Right of Kings*, 2nd edn, Cambridge, Cambridge University Press.

Ford, D. F. and Stamps, D. L. (eds), 1996. *Essentials of Christian Community: Essays for Daniel W. Hardy*, Edinburgh, T. & T. Clark.

Forrester, D. B., 1988. *Theology and Politics*, Oxford, Blackwell.

Forrester, D. B., 1999. 'Ecclesia Scoticana – Established, Free or National?', *Theology*, CII (1999), pp. 80–9.

General Synod, 1992. *Senior Church Appointments*, London, Church House Publishing.

Gierke, O., 1958 (1900). *Political Theories of the Middle Age*, tr. F. W. Maitland, Cambridge, Cambridge University Press.

Gill, R., 1981. *Prophecy and Praxis*, London, Marshall, Morgan & Scott.

Gladstone, W. E., 1841. *The State in Its Relation with the Church*, 4th edition, 2 vols, London.

Habgood, J., 1983. *Church and Nation in a Secular Age*, London, Darton, Longman & Todd.

Habgood, J., 1988. *Confessions of a Conservative Liberal*, London, SPCK.

Habgood, J., 1993. *Making Sense*, London, SPCK.

Hannaford, R. (ed.), 1998. *A Church for the Twenty-First Century*, Leominster, Gracewing.

Hastings, A., 1991. *Church and State: The English Experience (Prideaux Lectures 1990)*, Exeter, University of Exeter Press.

Hastings, A., 1997. *The Construction of Nationhood: Ethnicity, Religion and Nationalism*, Cambridge, Cambridge University Press.

Hazell, R. (ed.), 1999. *Constitutional Futures: A History of the Next Ten Years*, Oxford, Oxford University Press (The Constitution Unit).

Hazlitt, W., 1927. *Essays*, London, University Tutorial Press.

Hennessy, P., 1996. *The Hidden Wiring: Unearthing the British Constitution*, London, Indigo.

Henson, H. H., 1908. *The National Church*, London, Macmillan.

Henson, H. H., 1929. *Disestablishment*, London, Macmillan.

Henson, H. H., 1946. *Bishoprick Papers*, Oxford, Oxford University Press.

Hinchcliff, P., 1997. 'Colonial Church Establishment in the Aftermath of the Colenso Controversy' in N. Aston (ed.), 1997.

Hinton, M., 1994. *The Anglican Parochial Clergy*, London, SCM Press.

Hooker, R., 1845. *Works*, ed. J. Keble, 3 vols, Oxford, Oxford University Press.

Hutchinson, J. and Smith, A. D. (eds), 1994. *Nationalism*, Oxford and New York, Oxford University Press.

Jacob, W. M., 1997. *The Making of the Anglican Church Worldwide*, London, SPCK.

James, R. R., 1998. *A Spirit Undaunted: The Political Role of George VI*, London, Little, Brown and Co.

Kaye, B., 1996. *A Church Without Walls*, Victoria, Dove.

Lewis-Jones, J., 1999. *Reforming the Lords: The Role of the Bishops*, London, University College London: The Constitution Unit.

Macaulay, T. B., 1905 (1839). 'Gladstone on Church and State', *Essays*, London, Longmans, Green & Co.

McLeod, H., 1996. *Religion and Society in England 1850–1914*, Basingstoke, Macmillan.

Marr, A., 2000. *The Day Britain Died*, London, Profile.

Martin, D., 1969. *The Religious and the Secular*, London, Routledge.

Martin, D., 1993. *A General Theory of Secularization*, Aldershot, Gregg Revivals, (Oxford, Blackwell. 1978).

Martin, D., 1997. *Reflections on Sociology and Theology*, Oxford, Clarendon Press.

Matthew, H. C. G., 1997. *Gladstone 1809–1898*, Oxford, Clarendon Press.

Maurice, F., 1884. *Life of Frederick Denison Maurice*, 2 vols, London, Macmillan.

Maurice, F. D., 1958. *The Kingdom of Christ*, 2 vols, ed. A. Vidler, London, SCM Press.

Mikat, P., 1975. 'Church and State' in K. Rahner (ed.), *Encyclopedia of Theology*, London, Burns and Oates, pp. 227-37.

[Moberly], 1952. *Church and State*, London, Church Information Office.

Modood, T. (ed.), 1997. *Church, State and Religious Minorities*, London, Policy Studies Institute.

Moore, E. G., 1967. *An Introduction to English Canon Law*, Oxford, Clarendon Press.

Morris, C., 1989. *The Papal Monarchy: The Western Church from 1050 to 1250*, Oxford, Clarendon Press.

Moses, J., 1995. *A Broad and Living Way: Church and State, a Continuing Establishment*, Norwich, Canterbury Press.

Moyser, G. (ed.), 1985. *Church and Politics Today: The Role of the Church of England in Contemporary Politics*, Edinburgh, T & T Clark.

Nicholls, D., 1967. *Church and State in England since 1820* (Readings in Politics and Society), London, Routledge & Kegan Paul.

Nicholls, D., 1975. *The Pluralist State*, London and Basingstoke, Macmillan.

O'Brien, C. C., 1992. *The Great Melody: Edmund Burke*, London, Sinclair Stevenson (Minerva, 1993).

O'Donovan, O., 1996. *The Desire of the Nations: Rediscovering the Roots of Political Theology*, Cambridge, Cambridge University Press.

Palmer, B., 1992. *High and Mitred: Prime Ministers as Bishop-Makers 1837–1977*, London, SPCK.

Parker, T. M., 1955. *Christianity and the State in the Light of History*, London, A. & C. Black.

Parkin, C., 1956. *The Moral Basis of Burke's Political Thought*, Cambridge, Cambridge University Press.

Persenius, R., 1999. 'The Year 2000: Disestablishment in Sweden', *Theology*, CII (1999), pp. 177-86.

Pilgrim, W. E., 1999. *Uneasy Neighbours: Church and State in the New Testament*, Minneapolis, Fortress Press.

Pimlott, B., 1996. *The Queen: A Biography of Elizabeth II*, London, HarperCollins.

Platten, S. (ed.), 1999. *The Retreat of the State*, Norwich, Canterbury Press.

[Porvoo], 1993. *Together in Mission and Ministry: The Porvoo Common Statement*, London, Church House Publishing.

Raiser, K., 1999. 'That the World May Believe: The Missionary Vocation as the Necessary Horizon for Ecumenism', *International Review of Mission*, LXXXVIII (1999), pp. 187-96.

Robbers, G. (ed.), 1996. *State and Church in the European Union*, Baden Baden, Nomos Gesellschaft.

Sachs, W. L., 1993. *The Transformation of Anglicanism: From State Church to Global Communion*, Cambridge, Cambridge University Press.

Sedgwick, P., 1996. 'On Anglican Polity' in D. F. Ford and D. L. Stamps (eds), *Essentials of Christian Community: Essays for Daniel W. Hardy*, Edinburgh, T. & T. Clark.

[Selbourne], 1916. *Report of the Archbishops' Committee on Church and State*, London, SPCK.

Sell, A. P. F., 1985. 'Dubious Establishment: A Neglected Ecclesiological Testimony', *Mid-Stream*, XXIV (1985), pp. 1-28.

Shils, E., 1975. *Center and Periphery: Essays in Macrosociology*, Chicago and London, University of Chicago Press.

Spurr, J., 1991. *The Restoration Church of England 1646–1689*, London, Yale University Press.

Stanley, A. P., 1891. *The Life and Correspondence of Thomas Arnold D.D.*, 4th edn, London, Ward Lock.

Stanlis, P., 1958. *Edmund Burke and the Natural Law*, Ann Arbor, University of Michigan Press.

Sunkin, M. and Payne, S., 1999, *The Nature of the Crown*, Oxford, OUP.

Sykes, N., 1959. *From Sheldon to Secker: Aspects of English Church History 1660–1768*, Cambridge, Cambridge University Press.

Tappert, T. G. (ed.), 1959. *The Book of Concord*, Philadelphia, Fortress Press.

Ullmann, W., 1949. *Medieval Papalism: The Political Theories of the Medieval Canonists*, London, Methuen.

Ullmann, W., 1977. *Medieval Foundations of Renaissance Humanism*, London, Elek.

Varley, E. A., 1992. *The Last of the Prince Bishops: William Van Mildert and the High Church Movement of the Early Nineteenth Century*, Cambridge, Cambridge University Press.

Vidler, A. R., 1945. *The Orb and the Cross: A Normative Study in the Relations of Church and State with reference to Gladstone's Early Writings*, London, SPCK.

Ward, K., 1992. 'Is a Christian State a Contradiction?' in D. Cohn-Sherbok and D. McLellan (eds.), *Religion in Public Life*, Basingstoke and New York, St Martin's Press.

Watkin, T. G., 1998. 'Church and State in a Changing World' in N. Doe, M. Hill and R. Ombres (eds), *English Canon Law: Essays in Honour of Bishop Eric Kemp*, Cardiff, University of Wales Press.

Warren, A. (ed.), 1992. *A Church for the Nation?* Leominster, Gracewing.

Whitgift, J., *Works*, Parker Society edition of the works of the English Reformers, Cambridge, 1840–.

Williams, R. D., 1989. 'Postmodern Theology and the Judgement of the World' in F. B. Burnham (ed.), *Postmodern Theology: Christian Faith in a Pluralistic World*, San Francisco: Harper & Row.

Wolffe, J., 1994. *God and Greater Britain: Religion and National Life in Britain and Ireland 1843–1945*, London and New York, Routledge.

Young, F. (ed.), 1995. *Dare We Speak of God in Public?* London, Mowbray.

Index

Anglican Communion 7
Anglican-Methodist unity 9, 71,
    90–1
apostolicity of the church 2
Arnold, Thomas 54–6

Belgium 21
bishops 4; appointment 25, 28–30,
    34, 73; legal status 25;
    membership of House of
    Lords 20–1
Blomfield, C. J. 82
Bogdanor, Vernon 31
Burke, Edmund 30, 47–50

Calvin, John 44
canon law 25–7
Catholic Emancipation 64
catholicity of the Church 1–2
Church of England, numerical
    strength/decline 75–7
church unity 1–2, 8–10
Clements, Keith 80–1
Coleridge, Samuel Taylor 50–1
Constantine 40
constitutional monarchy 24
coronation 31–2
Cosin, John 28
Cranmer, Thomas 42, 43
Creighton, Mandell 58–9
Crown 24
Crown Appointments Commission 73

Dacre, Lord 30
Denmark 21
Diana, Princess of Wales 11
dioceses 4–5
disestablishment, effect on monarchy
    31; not advocated by 1936
    report 33; T. S. Eliot's view
    34
Dyson, Anthony 76

ecumenical movement 8, 67–8, 76
Eliot, T. S. 35
Erastianism 27
establishment, meaning of the term
    x–xi, 18–22, 87–8; positive
    case for 12–13

Figgis, J. N. 66–7
Finland 21
Forrester, Duncan 79
Forsyth, P. T. 69
Free Churches 69–70, 86

Germany 21
Gladstone, William Ewart 52–4, 82
globalization 7
Gore, Charles 65–6

Habgood, John 79
Henson, Hensley 31, 33–4, 66, 76
holiness 1
Hook, W. F. 66

Hooker, Richard 28, 45–7
House of Lords 20

Ireland 22, 64, 65
Israel, ancient 38

Jenkins, Daniel 69–70
Jewish emancipation 64

Kaye, Bruce 84

Lambeth Conference (1930) 14, 22
liberal view of the State 61
Luther, Martin 44

Macaulay, Lord 54
Maurice, F. D. 56–8
Melanchthon, Philip 43
Methodist Church 70–1
Mildert, Van 28, 64, 66
ministerial responsibility 24–5
mission viii, 1–2, 8–10, 62, 81–3, 87
monarch, as Supreme Governor of
    the Church of England 26,
    31, 65; *see also* constitutional
    monarchy; Royal Supremacy;
    sovereignty

national church, idea of 5, 6, 13–17,
    74–5
nationalism viii; *see also* sovereignty
nationhood 5–7, 88–9
New Testament 38–40

O'Donovan, Oliver 81
Old Testament 37–8

parishes 3
parliament *see* House of Lords;
    ministerial responsibility
Paul 39
pluralist society vii, viii–ix, 11, 47,
    53, 63–73
Prime Minister 73

Queen *see* monarch

registration of births and marriages
    65
Roman Catholic Church 7, 68–9
Royal Supremacy 23–4, 27, 42

Scotland 20, 64, 80, 86
secularization vii, 11, 61, 77–8
Sedgwick, Peter 83–4
sovereignty ix, 5, 24; of God 38
State, and government 60–1;
    see also monarch; nationhood;
    parliament
Sweden 19–20
Sykes, Norman 86

Thirty-Nine Articles 14, 23, 27

Ultramontanism 7, 69
United Reformed Church 71–2
unity of the church *see* church unity

Vatican City 68–9

Wales 22, 65, 80
Ward, Keith 78
Whitgift, John 43
Williams, Rowan 80